Growth Centres in Spatial Planning

Growth Centres in Spatial Planning

MALCOLM J. MOSELEY

Lecturer in Environmental Sciences
at the University of East Anglia

PERGAMON PRESS

Oxford · New York · Toronto · Sydney

Pergamon Press, Ltd., Headington Hill Hall, Oxford

Pergamon Press Inc., Maxwell House, Fairview Park, Elmsford, New York 10523

Pergamon of Canada Ltd., 207 Queen's Quay West, Toronto 1

Pergamon Press (Aust.) Pty. Ltd., 19a Boundary Street, Rushcutters Bay, N.S.W. 2011, Australia

First edition 1974

Library of Congress Cataloging in Publication Data

Moseley, Malcolm.
Growth centres in spatial planning.

Urban and regional planning series, v. 9)
Bibliography: p.
1. Regional planning. 2. Economic zoning.
3. Space in economics. I. Title. II. Series
HT391.M654   309.2′5   74-9962
ISBN 0-08-018055-8

**Urban and Regional Planning Series
Volume 9**

Printed in Great Britain by A. Wheaton & Co., Exeter

To my parents

Contents

Preface

AN EMPHASIS upon potential rather than need, efficiency rather than equity, concentration rather than dispersal, the long rather than the short term *and* an acceptance that these goals be pursued with sufficient moderation so that each broad region within a country may be seen to be benefiting— these are the essential elements of a growth-centre policy. Such a policy differs considerably from the alternatives of either *laissez-faire* or else "work to the workers" which most western countries practised 15 years ago. Today, virtually every advanced country, and several in the developing world too, practises a growth-centre policy—albeit in a variety of guises, to a varying degree and by an assortment of means. And yet this pursuit of "decentralised concentration", of deliberately fostering at the regional level a degree of spatial imbalance which is deemed unacceptable nationally, is founded upon premises which are rarely elaborated adequately and sometimes conflicting. Typically, growth centres are expected to achieve one or more of the following planning objectives: an improvement in a region's potential for adopting innovations; a programme of regional economic growth which is faster, greater or more assured than would otherwise have occurred; a saving in public investment on infrastructure; a more efficient pattern of service provision; a dissemination of growth impulses throughout the problem region; and the interception of would-be migrants from the region. This book is designed to question each assumption in turn. To what extent are growth-centre policies likely to attain the objectives? In what ways might such policies be modified in consequence?

At this stage it seems appropriate to confess four possible sources of "imbalance" of my own. To begin with, my first-hand experience of regional development policies has been confined to Western Europe. For 5 years I have been looking at the issue of "spatial discrimination" within Brittany and East Anglia, while attached to the universities of Rennes, Reading and East Anglia. This is not to say that the ensuing argument is inapplicable to planners outside the peripheral, essentially rural regions of advanced western countries with mixed economies—only that it has been this sort of context that has been the focus of my attention. Figure 1 sets out an "identikit" picture of the sort of region I have had in mind while writing.

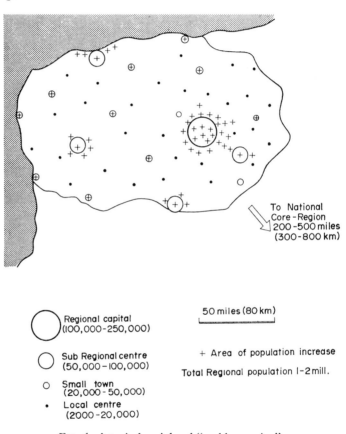

To National
Core - Region
200 -500 miles
(300-800 km)

⬭ Regional capital
(100,000-250,000)

○ Sub Regional centre
(50,000 - 100,000)

○ Small town
(20,000 - 50,000)

• Local centre
(2000 -20,000)

50 miles (80 km)

+ Area of population increase

Total Regional population 1-2 mill.

FIG. 1. A typical peripheral "problem region".

Second, as an academic, not a practising planner, my brief is to try to understand the real world, not to manipulate it. But Bertrand Russell once said that there is nothing more practical than a good theory: it is in this spirit that this book has been written and for this reason that I make no apology for dwelling on "academic" questions. The output is unfortunately not a "good theory" of growth centres: it would be premature to attempt that. But it seemed that the balance of advantages lay in trying to ask some basic questions properly, rather than in seeking to concoct a definitive "guide-book to growth centres" for the justifiably impatient planner.

Third, this is a work of synthesis, not analysis. A truly original thought is a rare commodity—there may not be a single one in the whole of this book! I have simply tried to pull together a widely scattered literature and to condense it, appraise it and reorganise it about a single theme—the value of growth-centre policies in spatial planning. This means, of course, that my debt to the original analysts—as well as to earlier synthesists—is enormous.

Fourth, and perhaps most significant, this book has been written by a geographer—someone wearing that particular pair of tinted spectacles which is designed to clarify, but hopefully not to magnify, the *spatial* element of the world's problems. The focus of modern geography is not a particular phenomenon, but a *dimension* (the spatial dimension) of "other people's" phenomena, be they essentially social, economic, political or whatever. Thus it does not constitute outdated academic protectionism to claim that the issue of the spatial distribution of activity is intrinsically geographical in its nature. But I have tried to bear constantly in mind the geographer's occupational hazard of exaggerating the importance of the spatial dimension in the world's problems and hence his ability to understand them fully. Though the spatial pattern of activity is intrinsically geographical, it is also of deep concern to other social scientists and to a wide variety of "change-agents" in the public and private sectors besides explicitly "spatial" planners, and it is for all these people that this book is intended.

Finally, I must acknowledge some of my more obvious debts. For kind permission to reproduce copyright material I am grateful to: The Controller of Her Majesty's Stationery Office for figures from *Central Scotland: A Programme for Development and Growth, The Central Borders: A Plan for Expansion,* and *Grangemouth/Falkirk Regional Survey and Plan;* the editor and publisher of the *Journal of Regional Science* for my Fig. 6.12; the East Anglia Economic Planning Council and East Anglian Consultative Committee for my Fig. 4.5, taken from the *Small Towns Study;* the Highlands and Islands Development Board for my Fig. 2.3, which is based on maps in the Board's *6th Annual Report*; to the publisher (Macmillan Publishing Co., Inc.) and editor (N. M. Hansen) of *Growth Centres in Regional Economic Development* for my Fig. 3.2; the editor and publisher of *Environment and Planning* for my Fig. 6.3; to Resources for the Future, Inc. for my Fig. 3.1, taken from *The Quality of the Urban Environment;* the editor and publisher of *Regional Studies* for my Figs. 6.4, 6.5, 6.6, 6.7, 6.8, 6.10, 6.11, which were previously published in Moseley (1973a and b); the editor of *Journal of the Town Planning Institute* for my Fig. 6.9.

For permission to include in Chapter 1 part of a paper published in 1973, I am grateful to the editor and publisher of *Area*. Dr P. A. Stone very kindly allowed me to read in draft a book which was subsequently published as Stone (1973).

This book was researched and written while I was engaged upon the Leverhulme "Movement of Industry" project in the Centre of East Anglian Studies at the University of East Anglia. I am grateful to the Leverhulme Trustees for their financial backing and to the secretary to the project team, Anita Schweinberger, for conscientiously typing the various working papers and drafts.

In addition, I must acknowledge my debt to A. A. L. Caesar and David Keeble at Cambridge and Peter Hall at Reading for stimulating my interest in the relationships between spatial distributions, economic development and regional planning. More recently, Morgan Sant, Peter Townroe and Margaret Camina, colleagues on the "Leverhulme Project", have contributed substantially by critical comment and encouragement. So too, in more modest ways, have many others too numerous to mention individually. I am grateful to them all.

Norwich   M. J. M.

CHAPTER 1

Growth-centre Theory and Growth-centre Policy

POLICIES of deliberately channelling growth to certain favoured places in order to achieve wider regional or national goals are now advocated or practised in a variety of countries, at different stages of development and with different political and economic systems. These favoured places have been variously termed growth (or development) poles, centres, points, areas, axes or nuclei. The justification and the expression of these policies is far from constant, but frequent reference is made to "growth-pole theory" as providing an underlying conceptual framework and *modus operandi* and it seems proper to begin this review of the validity of these discriminatory policies with an appraisal of that theory. Then follows a criticism of the growth-centre concept and the chapter concludes by introducing some of the fundamental issues which are involved in putting such policies into practice.

GROWTH-POLE THEORY

"Growth-pole theory" is certainly wide-ranging. Indeed, some would have it that it has at least the elements of the elusive, all-embracing general theory of regional development and planning. Hermansen tentatively suggests that "the theory can now be said to deal synthetically with the problem of societal development . . . in a simultaneous sectoral–spatial–temporal setting" (1972b, p. 1). He argues that "growth-pole theory" is an umbrella term, embracing a large number of more specific theories which are positive and normative; static and dynamic; sociological, economic and

1

Space	Time	
	Static	Dynamic
Geographic	Urban hierarchy and rank–size models Central place theory Traditional industrial location theory Network theory Optimum city-size theories Nodal regionalisation Gravity models	Centre-periphery and cumulative causation models Models of urban growth Agglomeration economies Spatial diffusion of innovations Activity allocation models
Economic	Input–output models Industrial complex analysis Pecuniary external economies Multiplier analysis	"Growth-pole" theory Leading and propulsive industries Diffusion of innovations among industries Programming of industrial complexes

Fig. 1.1. Some models and theories relating to "polarisation" (after Hermansen, 1972a).

geographical. The essence of the idea is that development is selective in its initial incidence (i.e. it is "polarised"), and that sociological, economic and geographical theories relating respectively, for example, to innovation diffusion, industrial complexes or central places are merely elaborating this idea in their respective disciplines or "dimensions". Figure 1.1, which draws on Hermansen (1972a), tabulates some of the related theories.

It was Francois Perroux of course who first coined the term "growth pole" (*pole de croissance*) (Perroux, 1955, 1964). However, in this book Perroux's work will not be considered at length—for two reasons. First, there is now an extensive literature reviewing his contribution and clarifying much of the fundamental confusion that arose from his simultaneous consideration of development in the social, economic and geographical dimensions.* Second, as was stated in the Preface, this is a book about the *locational* aspects of development, and the weakest aspect of Perroux's treatment of the process of development was his conception of poles as localities in geographic space (though ironically, and perhaps tragically, it is *this* conception of growth poles that has most frequently been incorporated into developmental policies).

Briefly, what seems to be the essence of Perroux's work, and of its relevance to the geographer and spatial planner? First, Perroux was concerned with development, not just growth: that is to say, he was concerned not just with quantitative expansion, but with the process of structural change as well. Second, his focus was "multi-dimensional" in that he was concerned with growth and structural change in social systems, in the economy and in geographical space as well. Third, Perroux had a novel conception of "space", within which development occurs. He wrote (1950, p. 91) that there are "as many spaces as there are structures of abstract relations which define an object". Irrespective of whether the object in question be essentially economic (e.g. a certain industry), organisational (e.g. a business firm) or geographical (e.g. a town) it could be studied in its "planning space" which defines the domain within which its plans are formulated, "homogeneous space" which defines the extent of similar objects, and "space as a field of forces" which defines the extent of other objects which act upon it. Fourth, with regard to "space as a field of forces", with which he was mainly concerned, Perroux claimed that development

---

*Recent reviews of the "multi-dimensional" aspects of Perroux's ideas include those by Darwent (1969) and Thomas (1972).

was unbalanced: it took place first at key nodes, from which developmental impulses spread to other objects, but which, being themselves best placed for further development, were likely to become cumulatively more developed. In other words, Perroux championed the idea of imbalance in development, in marked contrast to the equilibrium notions of more traditional economists, geographers and sociologists. Fifth, Perroux (following Schumpeter) stressed that it is the propensity of these key nodes to adopt innovations that assures their development. Innovations, new ideas, new processes are the driving force of development, and are most easily adopted at the foci of these fields of forces, in whatever space. Sixth, certain of these nodes or foci, because of their large size, high degree of connectivity, high rate of innovation adoption and rate of growth are able to so dominate the objects with which they are linked that they, the dominant nodes, effectively control the latter's rate of development. Such dominant nodes he termed "growth poles".

Now, Perroux's particular contribution was that he applied the temporal notion of development simultaneously in social, economic and geographic spaces. And, if the last paragraph is sufficiently clearly written, an economist concerned with firms and industries, or a sociologist con-concerned with organisations, or a geographer concerned with spatial agglomerations should each be able to apply its content in the context of his own discipline. But the key question for the geographer and spatial planner is just how far Perroux's hypotheses do in fact conform to the geographical dimension of the real world, for it is clear that Perroux was not primarily interested in geographical space (he called it "banal"). And when he wrote "growth does not appear everywhere all at once: it appears in points or growth poles with varying intensity: it spreads via various channels and with varying effects . . ." (1964, p. 143), we must beware of jumping to a geographical interpretation of the words "growth pole" and "everywhere": Perroux had a very comprehensive view of space.

There are two different ways in which the relevance of the growth-pole notion, to the geographer and spatial planner, has been conceived. The first is to seek out an object or node which apparently has growth-pole characteristics in *all* spaces—including geographical space. Thus Hermansen, referring specifically to the structure of geographical space, wrote (Hermansen, 1972b, pp. 29–30): "Not every centre of a nodal region qualifies to be called a development pole. Only those which contain propulsive firms—i.e. large-scale firms, technically advanced, innovating and dominating, and working within propulsive industries (industries with a marked capacity for inducing growth in linked industries) which exert a strong influence on their environment and are capable of generating sustained growth over a prolonged period of time—should be regarded as geographical poles of growth." Thus Hermansen argued that true geographical growth poles must contain growth-pole *firms* within growth-pole *industries*. In other words, the argument is that growth poles on the ground are the geographical expression of propulsive firms and industries. And, as a corollary, growth-pole policies involve the grouping geographically of firms and industries, which are propulsive in all other spaces at the same time. I would argue, however, that this interpretation unnecessarily reduces the number of "true geographical growth poles" to a very small number, and, more important, has potentially dangerous implications for regional planning. It opens the way for policies of grouping together growth-pole firms and industries (those big, innovative, well-connected objects which "dominate" economic and organisational space) in the belief that they will necessarily engender *localised* development through the dissemination of their development impulses within neighbouring parts of their geographical field of forces (or "nodal region"). This belief has frequently produced "cathedrals in the desert"—industrial complexes whose developmental impulses are real enough, but which are channelled to linked firms and industries hundreds of miles away.

A second role for the growth-pole model in geographical theory is to treat it as an "analogue model"—i.e. to accept, as Perroux implied, that its tenets are mainly applicable in economic and organisational space, but to examine them closely to see if they provide stimulating hypotheses for translation to the geographical dimension. This would draw our attention to nodal locations, and their role in the development process. Such nodal locations are almost always towns or wider urban areas, given the marked mutual reinforcement of accessibility and urbanisation. So, following from the growth-pole model, we are led to examine the degree to which development is geographically unbalanced, with urban areas becoming progressively more developed. We examine the degree to which towns dominate their hinterlands, and the role of their spatial connectivity, their size, growth-rate and propensity to adopt innovations in this domination. Indeed, following Perroux, we are forced to concentrate closely on the role of innovations in the developmental process, and the pattern of their transmission. We are led to examine the channels by which "growth impulses" are transmitted from towns to their nodal regions. But most important, if we accept the role of growth-pole theory as an analogue *model* for spatial analysis, we are forced to remember that any supposed parallels between growth poles in geographical space and those in other spaces must be treated as *unproven* hypotheses, for testing in the real world. It is for this reason that Perroux's work does not itself provide material for examining the validity of (geographical) growth-pole policies, and that we must look to other, more specifically locational, theories to explain the process of development in that dimension. Thus the argument in this book is that growth-pole theory has little *direct* relevance to the geographical pattern of development, that assertions of propulsive industries and industrial complexes being directly relevant to regional development are highly questionable, and that it is necessary to turn directly to locational theories if we are to understand the geographical pattern and process of development.

Two further points, on semantics, should be made at this stage. First, to retain the term "growth pole" for propulsive nodes in geographical as well as the other spaces would seem to court unnecessary confusion. Consequently, following Darwent (1969), we use the term "growth centre" for the geographical entity. In this book the term "growth pole" will not be used again in a geographical context, except in quotations from other writers. Second, having completed our brief review of Perroux and his comprehensive conception of "space", henceforth the words "space" and "spatial" will be reserved exclusively for geographical or topological space. Thus the words "spatial" and "geographical" will henceforth be considered to be synonymous in this book.

We must turn, therefore, to location theory to understand the spatial pattern and process of development, but what we find is not entirely satisfactory. Traditional theories of the location of central places and of industry sought to explain the spatial patterns of service and manufacturing activity respectively but in an essentially static context. While central place theory elegantly explains the typical spacing, size and hierarchy of settlements, it says little about how the system is likely to react to the onset of further development initially taking place in only one, or a few of those settlements. And not only is it not dynamic, but by assuming in a very deterministic way that all locational decisions made by the firms concerned are designed to maximise profits, and that all business-men are fully informed and rational in their decision-making, it abstracts from reality to a degree which further reduces its value for studies of the process of development. Indeed, as we are concerned with change and development, there is a strong case for following Richardson (1973a) in accepting the present pattern of settlements as given "locational constants" and focusing our attention on theories which explain the progressive modification of that pattern.

Perhaps the most useful dynamic theories in economic geography are those which incorporate ideas of cumulative causation, and the tendency for initial disparities to be accentuated. These theories, with which the names of Hirschman (1958), Myrdal (1957) and Friedman (1969) are associated, and which are discussed in detail below (Chaps. 5 and 6), draw heavily on the real or supposed benefits and costs of agglomeration, in order to explain the progressive clustering of economic activities, and the possibility of spread at a later stage. And Friedmann in particular, whose "general theory of polarised development" attempts to "explain systematic interrelations between development and space, a theory in other words of the development process in its spatial dimension" (1969, p. 1), assigns crucial importance to the capacity of a centre to generate or adopt innovations. So the diffusion of innovations, as Perroux suggested, warrants close attention in our consideration of the spatial dimension of development. Fortunately geographers have produced a quite well-developed theory on this subject.

The basic elements of a dynamic theory of spatial development certainly exist, but, unfortunately, it remains true that theories of regional economic development and theories of spatial structure have developed largely independently of each other. The latter have been generally static and devoid of developmental elements, and the former have tended to draw heavily on neoclassical theory, with regions being treated as mere points in space, their development resting largely on the movement of labour and capital in response to wage and capital yield differentials. Today, attempts are being made to draw the two together, with Richardson (1973a), in particular, claiming that the spatial structure of a region and the size and spacing of its towns may be the crucial factors in explaining regional growth potential. Clearly this recent thrust in regional economics is closely akin to growth-centre ideas of regional development. Each places great emphasis on the "geographical incongruence between supply and demand of resources" (Parr, 1972a) as a factor hindering development, and calls for a remarshalling of the capital and labour resources of a region into a pattern suitable for the attraction, generation and sustenance of new economic activity.

THE GROWTH-CENTRE CONCEPT*

We have argued so far that "growth-pole theory" provides the stimulating hypothesis that development is polarised in geographical space around nodes which we may call "growth centres". It has also been argued that other bodies of theory, specifically devoted to the geographical dimension, must be used to elaborate and refine this idea. But even if we jettison the "growth pole" into the realm of economics and sociology, it is arguable whether there remains a generally accepted and readily appreciated geographical entity which can be safely termed "growth centre". Examination of the use of this term (or of "growth pole" when explicitly used in a geographical sense) and of attempts to identify such phenomena in the real world reveals a great deal of residual confusion and disagreement.

What is at issue is whether the growth centre is a real entity or an abstract construct. To begin with, few authors give an explicit definition of the term, and where definitions are attempted they are clearly not consistent one with another. Consider the following four:

> . . . an urban core (however small) and its surrounding area defined by an acceptable journey-to-work, and capable either of spontaneous growth—both of population, economic activity and income level together—or of potential growth (which could, if required, be stimulated by government intervention). Another important feature . . . is that the benefits of its growth are likely to be felt also in the surrounding area. (EFTA, 1968, p. 21.)

> A main centre at the regional level which, in addition to its function as a regional service centre, also provides a prosperous and reasonably diversified industrial structure. The centre should either be growing or show potential for growth of economic activity, employment, population and income. Such a centre will, *ceteris paribus*, need to be above a certain population level, or if it is to enjoy self-sustaining growth, be planned for such a level. (Allen and Hermansen, 1968, p. 64.)

---

*This section draws heavily on the author's "Growth centres—a shibboleth?", published in *Area* (1973), **5**, 2, pp. 143–50.

. . . an urban place of less than 250,000 population which acts as the vital heart of its development district (Fox, 1966, p. i). (Fox then lists as relevant criteria strong linkage to the national economy, the centre of a labour market, a major retail trade area, high-level tertiary functions, a large volume of whole-sale trade and good communications.)

. . . . an urban centre of economic activity which can achieve self-sustaining growth, to the point that growth is diffused outward into the pole region and eventually beyond into the less developed region of the nation. (Nichols, 1969, p. 193.)

Such definitions contain recurrent themes, relating for example to urban status, size, functional role, location and growth, but the emphasis varies and few authors explain the relative importance of the characteristics they list. And so, from rather extravagant assemblies of supposedly interrelated attributes, it is very difficult to single out the irreducible minimum, the *sine qua non* of the concept. In fact, most writers seem to be describing their mental picture of a growth centre, without considering whether their picture represents a meaningful entity. All this is closely analogous to the geographer's old dilemma: do *regions* "exist" in the real world, or are they abstract constructs? It is not an arid point: if growth centres do not con-stitute a "species" of places, then it may be less confusing to speak, for example, of "central places" or "manufacturing towns", with any additional attributes, e.g. growth, clearly specified.

Figure 1.2 examines thirteen examples of the use of the term "growth centre" (or "pole", if employed geographically). The writers considered were each reporting some empirical work, not just reviewing previous use of the term or its application in regional planning. The table reveals the manner in which each resolved certain basic issues of interpretation. It is true that many explicitly recognised these dilemmas. It is also true that error and perhaps injustice may have been introduced—but the very difficulty of constructing this table is itself a comment on the depth of con-fusion which still exists.

At least seven basic issues, or groups of issues, emerge.

(i) *Growth or Centrality?*

Which of the two words comprising "growth centre" is crucial to the concept, or are they both? Opinions differ (cols. 3 and 4, Fig. 1.2). Fox (1966) and Carol (1966) place great store by the existence of high-level

Source	Term employed: Growth....	Explicit definition?	"Centrality" stressed?	"Growth" stressed?	Growth of what?	Timing of relevant attributes	Positive or normative?	Size (population)
Boudeville (1966)	Pole	Yes, p. 11	Yes	Yes	Industry	Present	Positive	> 15,000
Carol (1966)	Centre, pole (synonymous)	No	Yes	No	—	Present	Normative	—
Hodge (1966)	Centre, pole (synonymous)	No	Yes	Yes	Population, commercial facilities, infrastructure, manufacturing, incomes	Past and present	Normative	—
Fox (1966)	Centre	No	Yes	No	—	Present	Normative	< 250,000
Allen and Hermansen (1968)	Centre	Yes, p. 64	Yes	Yes	Economic activity, incomes, employment, population	Present or future	Both	30,000–250,000
Nichols (1969)	Pole	Yes, p. 139	No	Yes	—	Present or future	Both	Large enough for self-sustaining growth
Kuehn and Bender (1969)	Centre	No	No	Yes	Employment	Past	Normative	—
Casetti, King and Odland (1970)	Pole	Yes, p. 39	No	Yes	Employment	Past	Positive	—
Tolosa and Reiner (1970)	Pole	Yes, p. 451	Yes	Yes	Industry	Past and present	Both	—
Robinson and Salih (1971)	Pole	No	Yes	Yes	Economic development	Past and present	Positive	—
Bylund (1972)	Centre	No	Yes	No	—	Present	Normative	—
Lewis and Prescott (1972)	Centre	No	No	Yes	Public investment, population, economic activity	Past	Both	25,000–100,000
Misra (1972)	Centre	No	Yes	No	—	Present	Normative	50,000–500,000

Fig. 1.2. Interpretations of "growth centres" or geographical-type "growth poles".

(Note: Taken from my earlier paper "Growth centres—a shibboleth?" in *Area* 5, 2, (1973) pp. 143–50).

tertiary functions, while Kuehn and Bender (1969) are concerned only with economic growth. Allen and Hermansen (1968) suggest that both should be present. Of course, centrality and growth are often mutually reinforcing, but they may not be, so some decision seems necessary.

(ii) *The Nature of Centrality*

The term centrality has at least two connotations. It relates to intra-regional location or "nodality", measured by various indices of connectivity, and to central place function, indicated by the range of services provided, and there is no consistent opinion on their relative importance to the concept. Again they will probably, but not necessarily, be mutually reinforcing.

(iii) *The Nature of Growth*

Three points are important here. First, if growth is intrinsic to the concept, then growth of what? (col. 5). Some writers appear to mean growth "generally"; others are more specific, but are either all-embracing and so violate parsimony (e.g. Hodge, 1966) or else more particular, but not forthcoming on the reasons for their choice. Yet, clearly, there may be relatively little correspondence, particularly at the micro-scale, between the spatial patterns of growth in employment, industrial output, population, gross incomes, *per capita* incomes, etc. Second, do we mean absolute increments of growth or growth rates? Quite different spatial patterns are likely to emerge on the basis of this decision. The former will probably accord growth-centre status to the largest regional centres, the latter to certain small towns which have the advantage of growing from a small base. Third, how much growth? If, as is usual, growth *rates* are preferred, then against what base-line are rates compared (regional average, national average?), and by what amount should the growth rates of growth centres exceed that base-line?

(iv) *The Timing of Growth*

"Are we speaking of places or phenomena that have grown, that are growing (or) that are predicted to grow?" (Darwent, 1969, p. 5). Thus, while it may be permissible to say that a place is, was or will be a growth centre, it is not clear whether a place is a growth centre *now* on the grounds of its past or predicted performance. Obviously, data availability frequently necessitates a historical interpretation for empirical work (col. 6), but is pragmatism the main consideration? And for how long must a place grow in order to earn growth-centre status? Is a short spurt of growth sufficient, or must growth be sustained? What do we mean by sustained?

(v) *Positive or Negative?*

Is the growth centre a "positive" concept, aiding our understanding of the real world, or is it essentially "normative", i.e. a prescription for planning policy? Some interpretations contain normative elements: note, for example, the use in the definitions given above of such words as "acceptable", "if required" and "need to be". The logical extension of defining the concept in such terms appears to be that growth centres may comprise any places thus designated by the planner. And the irony of mixing normative and positive terms in the definition is that it rules out the objective analysis of growth centres upon which such policy should properly be based.

(vi) *The Problem of Scale*

Is the size of a place (however measured) relevant to its having growth-centre status? Where writers have indicated upper or lower limits, these are indicated in Fig. 1.2 (col. 8). More usual, however, is an assertion, more or less explicit, that growth centres are medium-sized, not too big and not too small, perhaps mid-way between "core regions" and "rural growth points" and enjoying some of the advantages of each. What is not clear is how great a range of places may be subsumed within one "species". If the Venezuelan "core region" around Caracas (Friedmann, 1966) and the small Scottish "growth point" of Lochaber (Turnock, 1966) are not in essence comparable, then where do valid break points occur? Some authors refer to a hierarchy of growth centres (sometimes with places in the top tier being confusedly termed "growth poles" (e.g. Misra, 1972)). Others restrict the term "growth centre" to places large enough to enjoy "self-sustaining" growth (e.g. Nichols, 1969) though this rather begs the questions of whether the self-sustenance of growth is a function primarily of urban size, and if so whether there exists a crucial size threshold beyond which growth has a disproportionately greater likelihood of being self-sustaining—an issue taken up in Chapter 5.

(vii) *Areal Extent*

But "mass" is not the only relevant "scale" parameter. If we say that a growth centre is located in geographic space, then it remains to define the latter's extent. Most writers consider the "centre" as no more than the built-up urban area, and go on to discuss the centre's spatial impact as an important, but separate, phenomenon. However, the EFTA definition, above, includes the urban area's journey-to-work hinterland as part of the growth centre itself—an approach which seems more in accord with the reality of urban systems. But two problems arise. First if we accept the systemic approach, then how do we adjudicate between the possible criteria for measuring the extent of the hinterland? Why not shopping or migration fields, or the pattern of industrial linkage instead of journey-to-work? Second, however we define the hinterland there is a danger of pre-judging hypotheses which relate to the ability of growth centres to transmit development impulses to that hinterland. Until and unless such hypotheses are proven, it may be better to content ourselves with a definition restricted to the built-up area, inadequate systemically though that is.

We now turn from the plethora of attempts to describe (if not define) growth centres to the much smaller number of attempts to identify them in the real world. (This step necessarily excludes interpretations of the concept which are wholly normative in that they set out attributes that growth centres "ought" to have.) Such attempts are few in number: the author knows of less than a dozen in a voluminous literature (see the bibliographies by Storey, 1972, and Davy, 1973). Each attempt is unique, and both their fewness and their uniqueness reaffirm the general argument that a universally acceptable interpretation of the term does not exist.

Some identification procedures are based on indices of centrality. Of these, Carol's (1966) is the most simple. The growth "poles" he identifies in southern Ontario are simply high- and middle-order central places as defined by the level of their retail sales. Tolosa and Reiner (1970) prefer a nodality interpretation of centrality and advocate the spatial analysis of economic and information flows and the application of graph theory to identify nodes or vertices in those flows. Vertices with above-average growth rates are then termed growth "poles". In a similar way Boudeville (1966) employed telephone-call data, but more with the intention of defining the extent of polarised regions than of identifying the centres upon which they focused.

Two other attempts are based on the requirement that growth centres stimulate further growth in their hinterlands. Semple *et al.* (1972) sought growth centres within the state of São Paulo, using composite indices of growth relating to each centre in that state. Their objective was to identify a centre such that the reciprocals of the distance from it to each of the other centres were positively and significantly correlated with the growth rates of those centres. In other words, they hypothesised that the state's surface of growth resembled a series of interlocking cones, and they used trend surface analysis to find the peaks of those cones. The procedure used by Casetti *et al.* (1970, 1971) was similar. But the authors began with the hypothesis that Los Angeles was the dominant growth centre in western USA, and tested its ability to influence the growth rates over 18 years of twelve cities within 1000 miles of it, using regression analysis. Proximity to Los Angeles clearly played a significant role, and so the former's growth-centre status was confirmed.

All of the other known attempts to identify growth centres focus primarily on the growth of the candidate town itself. Kuehn and Bender (1969) examining 125 counties in the Ozarks subjected the employment change occurring in each of the thirty-two economic sectors to shift and share analysis. The "composition" and "component" elements of this variation, plus the sums of those elements, were tabulated to give a 125×66 matrix. Each county's 66 scores were then correlated with those of each of the other counties in turn, and when the 124 correlation coefficients of each county were summed, those with the lowest totals were revealed as having undergone unusually great structural change and were termed growth centres. Thus, the technique is, as the authors admit, "merely a device for describing and comparing the changing employment structure of small geographic areas" (p. 437).

The other growth-based procedures are all multivariate exercises employing factor or principal components analysis in some way. Hodge (1966, 1968) condensed the variance expressed by thirty-two social, economic and physical variables relating to eighty towns in eastern Ontario into seven underlying dimensions, which were then incorporated as independent variables in multiple regression equations attempting to explain the growth performance of those towns. But although he entitles his earliest paper *"The Identification of 'Growth Poles' . . ."*, he did, in fact, go no further than to present the results of the preceding analysis to the policy-maker, declaring that the actual selection had to consider the question "growth for what purpose?" and was therefore a task for the politician rather than the analyst. Berry (1969) factor-analysed the economic structure of 105 Chilean towns, separately for 1952 and for 1960. Grouping these towns on the basis of their scores on the major factors, he identified five groups in each of the 2 years. Those towns which "moved up a group" between 1952 and 1960 he termed growth centres. Weinand (1969, 1973) examined the spatial pattern of development in Nigeria via a principal components analysis of ten relevant indices, relating to thirty-three regions. He identified what he termed an "entrepreneurship" component, loading highly on variables which measured the incidence of motor vehicles, telephone lines, wholesale and retail activities, banking and marketing. High scores on this component were said to reveal growth poles.

Hodge, Berry and Weinand each included both static and dynamic variables. The present author undertook principal component analyses exclusively of dynamic variables in his search for growth centres in East Anglia and in Brittany (Moseley, 1972). For each region variables were tabulated relating to migration, population change, dwelling construction, industrial expansion, employment change by sector, etc. For each region two significant components emerged which could be termed "general growth" and "recent industrialisation". Places scoring highly on both components were termed growth centres. Then, from among the centres which emerged, three were chosen (Rennes in Brittany, Thetford and Haverhill in East Anglia) as a basis for analyses of their spatial impact (Moseley, 1972, 1973a, b).

Thus, Hodge, Berry, Weinand and Moseley all employed a similar multivariate technique, but each sought growth centres in a quite different way: Hodge by trying to relate growth to his components, Berry by performing two analyses and considering the change which occurred in the intervening period, Weinand by focusing on the products of economic growth at a single point in time and Moseley by incorporating nothing but dynamic indices. But the truly *ad hoc* nature of these procedures derives only partially from their uniqueness: it derives also from the nature of the technique employed. The initial selection of "relevant" variables and their expression (e.g. growth rates or absolute increments?), the selection of "significant" components and their identification, the designation of "high" scores on these components—all were to some extent arbitrary decisions. Further, the irregularity of the shape and extent of the data blocks and the unavoidable under- and overbounding of towns, and the consequent exclusion or dilution respectively of the growth elements of these towns, added further to the arbitrariness of the exercises. It is clear that what came out depended very much upon what went in! (Figure 1.3 illustrates, for a hypothetical region, some of the possible identification procedures.)

Turning briefly to attempts to recommend the criteria upon which areas for designation as growth centres should be identified, a similar picture of overlap but uniqueness is apparent. The EFTA report (1968, pp. 66–67) sets out five prime indices: an increase in *per capita* income equal to or greater than the national average, an increase in gross income greater than the national average, substantial investment and production expansion, a rapid rate of increase in total population, and sufficient size to support a wide range of services. In addition, three extra factors are added though the authors admit the difficulty of operationally defining them: they are high potential for self-sustaining growth, for spilling growth into the neighbouring region and for integrating the region into the national economy.

An example of an attempt to apply certain indices in practice is that of the Appalachian Regional Commission (Ryan, 1970). As a condition of receipt of certain federal investment, the ARC required each of the thirteen Appalachian states to designate suitable growth centres, paying attention to location, labour resources, past growth performance and local financial viability. The states were permitted themselves to define and to weight these indices, and in fact they employed a variety of *ad hoc* methods. That the exercise produced 213 centres containing 80% of the population is an indication, perhaps, of the vagaries of the political process. Finally Milne (1970), dissatisfied with such official procedures, recommended use of the following criteria for the identification of growth centres in six problem regions of the United States: SMSA status, rapid

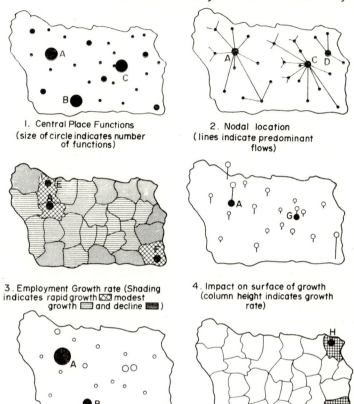

1. Central Place Functions
(size of circle indicates number
of functions)

2. Nodal location
(lines indicate predominant
flows)

3. Employment Growth rate (Shading
indicates rapid growth ⊠ modest
growth ⊟ and decline ▨)

4. Impact on surface of growth
(column height indicates growth
rate)

5. Absolute increase in population
(size of circle indicates number of
extra people)

6. Changing economic structure
(shaded areas have radically changed
their structure)

Fig. 1.3. Some ways of identifying "growth centres" in a hypothetical
region.

Growth centres emerging:
Map 1: High order central place facilities—towns A, B, C (after Carol,
1966).
Map 2: Nodal locations, using graph theory—towns A, C, D (after
Tolosa and Reiner, 1970).
Map 3: Employment growth rate—town A, town F (which grew from
a small base) and the suburban area E to the north of A.

employment growth, high intra-regional immigration and marked *per capita* income growth. Taking just these three proposals, the only criteria in any way common are growth and size, but these are interpreted in very different ways.

It is clear that we are still far from a universally acceptable definition of the growth-centre concept, and even further from a generally applicable identification procedure. The reader expecting the author to conclude this theoretical discussion by revealing what growth centres *really* are must remain disappointed! At the very least, there exists serious semantic confusion, but if this is all then given time and more discipline we should arrive at the true essence of the concept and the problem will disappear. This conclusion, the semantic interpretation of our difficulties, may, however, be too optimistic.

If there are as many interpretations of the concept as there are interpreters, then could not the problem be essentially a philosophical one? Perhaps growth centres, like the tree in Bishop Berkeley's quadrangle, exist only in the eye of the beholder? Certainly the various perceptions of growth centres overlap—ideas of growth, centrality, scale, and regional propulsion occur again and again—but the perceptions seem nonetheless to be unique and strictly personal. If this interpretation were the correct one, then two things would appear to follow. For the analyst, it would be as fruitful to seek the real essence of the concept as for a dog to chase his tail: neither could capture a quarry attached to himself. And for the planner, it would be spurious to designate growth centres in the belief that their attributes could be derived from a neatly bundled theory, and that their establishment would necessarily bring forth a package of desirable good things in the region. Both the analyst and the planner would have their growth centres made-to-measure, because they certainly do not come ready-to-wear.

Map 4: Significant impact on the surface of growth—town A, and town G which has only a moderate growth rate itself, but which lies (unliketown F) at the centre of a "cone" of modest growth after Semple *et al.*, 1972).

Map 5: Absolute increase in population—towns A and B.

Map 6: Changing economic struture—town F which has rapidly developed a small but diversified industrial base, and rural area H which has shifted from agriculture and fishing to tourism (after Kuehn and Bender, 1969).

Thus in this example, no town emerges as a growth centre in every analysis. But eight places qualify at least once. Are there any *true* growth centres?

To say that there is no clear object which may be unequivocally termed a "growth centre" may seem a strange conclusion with which to begin a book on the subject! But it seems the only reasonable conclusion. Nevertheless, it may be useful to give a working "definition" which is made-to-measure for the task in hand, that of examining just what attributes really do accompany urban growth: "A town which has recently experienced, or is presently experiencing or is planned to experience rapid growth." This "definition" begs most of the questions set out above and does so quite deliberately.

GROWTH-CENTRE POLICIES

The nebulous character of growth-centre theory has undoubtedly been one factor behind its widespread adoption in regional planning. Its breadth and flexibility introduce a vagueness which makes policies of discrimination easier to accept. It may be that the term has provided an expedient way, in many cases, of continuing pro-urban policies. But the basic implication of "steering a middle course", which underlies growth-centre policies, probably accounts for a larger proportion of its popularity—a middle course between concentration and dispersal, efficiency and equity, growth and welfare. It is clear that ideas of "concentrated decentralisation" have appeared attractive in a wide range of contexts.

The point is that many countries, irrespective of their level of development, have increasingly become sensitive to a syndrome of problems crudely but succinctly expressed as "apoplexy in the centre and anaemia at the edges". On the one hand, they have what seems to be excessive growth of their major city or cities with all the attendant extra costs to society that this apparently brings. On the other hand, they have regions, often peripherally located, with much slower rates of growth, lower levels of employment and *per capita* incomes and a degree of outmigration which seems to accentuate the problems of each set of regions. These "distressed regions" may have been once industrialised, but by industries now in decline, or they may be relatively sparsely populated, largely agricultural regions—the essence of the dichotomy remains the same. What could be more sensible than trying to create within the latter regions some of the metropolitan advantages of the former so that growth of employment and population would be stimulated in the latter, and in consequence curtailed in the former ? Without pronouncing on the wisdom of the diagnosis of the problem, it seems fair to say that this has been the most common argument put forward for growth-centre policies—i.e. that if growth is to be *effectively* promoted in distressed areas, then concentration of investment is required to provide the necessary environment for it.

But there have been other reasons suggesting the wisdom of concentrating any development diverted from the core region of the country into one or only a few chosen places. One idea is that because of economies of scale in the provision of public investment on "infrastructure", it is more efficient to concentrate. A second is that if innovation adoption is at the root of development, and if innovations are adopted most readily in the stimulating climate of large centres, then again the channelling of investment to the largest centres in a region appears advisable. Third, if migrants from the distressed region are to be diverted from the "core areas", and if possible intercepted in the region of origin, then again large centres in the latter region are required. Fourth, if the level and sophistication of services and amenities now required apparently ubiquitously are to be provided in the region of residence, then again large centres must be promoted because of the high (and rising) thresholds of support population required. Finally, given the political realities which require development to be spread widely within the distressed region, then faith in the spread effects of growth centres will again suggest as optimal a policy of initial concentration in order to build up a "cake" which will then be naturally shared out across the region.

So there are a wide range of objectives that have been put forward for justifying policies of promoting greater spatial concentration of resources in problem regions than would naturally occur—a policy which may be termed a "growth-centre policy". It is the ability of such policies to attain such objectives with which this book is concerned. But before this appraisal is undertaken it is necessary to look more closely at growth-centre policies: first, in this chapter at some basic issues which underlie policies of deliberate spatial discrimination and then, in the next chapter, at the actual form of such policies as practised in three specific countries. These issues will be considered under three headings—

(i) *Place Prosperity or People Prosperity?*

A basic point, sometimes forgotten in spatial planning, is that all objectives must be human objectives—they must be concerned with providing people's needs and wants. Being inanimate things, "places" have no objectives; they are the tools with which planners work—the means, not the ends. Thus Hoover (1969) has written that "the only legitimate final aim of public policy is to improve the welfare of people rather than areas of such" (p. 350). Now this leads clearly on to the rationale of spatial discrimination that although *people* should be helped according to their needs, this is best done if *places* are helped according to their *potential*—so long as a series of assumptions is met.

The first assumption is that "the people" are not totally immobile, through irrevocably wanting to "stay put" where they live. The second is that employment opportunities (or "industry") are not rendered totally immobile by the attractions of the core region of the country. The third and fourth assumptions are the converse of these, that neither "the people" nor "industry" is so mobile that it is willing and able to move in sufficient quantity all the way to the other. If these assumptions are met, and there seems a lot of evidence in favour of them, then the objective of helping people according to their needs seems to be in accordance with promoting growth in a few (the best) locations within their broad region of residence. And it has to be remembered that not only is an overtly "place prosperity" policy unlikely to be fully viable, but the people eventually aided in this way might not be those for whom concern was originally expressed. A place does not contain a fixed set of people.

(ii) *The Selection of Areas*

It is relatively easy in theory to advocate spatially discriminatory policies, but harder to put discrimination into practice in a way that is both politically acceptable and economically effective. The optimal selection of areas or centres will have to balance immediate need against growth potential, as discussed above, and will require clear definition and weighting of the factors indicating potential. But more than this, a decision will be needed on how far, between the extremes of concentration and dispersal, attention should be focused. Should "growth centres" be established in most problem areas, with discrimination being practised only between, on the one hand, the central small town and, on the other, the villages and truly rural areas? Or should all centres with fewer than, say, 200,000 inhabitants be ignored, with all that this implies for the extensive areas and the numerous smaller towns which separate them? So we have here a number of interlocking issues—how many growth centres?, how widely spaced? and which centres in particular?

(iii) *Implementation of the Policy*

Having decided on the wisdom of assisting places according to their potential, and having selected specific areas or centres to be favoured, how is the policy to be put into practice? First, what kind of growth? What is to be the nature of the export sector which will earn the income to support local services? Manufacturing or service? Labour- or capital-intensive? This sector or that . . . ?, etc. Second, by what means is it to be attracted? And, a more sensitive issue, how far should implementation of these means be itself spatially discriminatory? Should incentives be restricted only to firms establishing specifically in the growth centre, or should the whole problem region be afforded preferential status, with reliance being placed on the indirect advantages of the growth centre (its agglomeration economies) to lure the firms to the chosen place? (British practice has tended to favour the latter course.) Third, are complementary policies needed to stimulate labour mobility—to induce workers to commute or migrate to the growth centre? And what policies are needed for those who stay behind—in the form of welfare policies perhaps?

So "growth-centre policy" is no more cut-and-dried than is "growth-centre theory". Policies which go under this broad umbrella term are practised for a variety of reasons, in a variety of forms. But there do seem common threads—ideas of place potential rather than place need, of growth rather than distribution, of concentration rather than dispersal and, perhaps most important of all, the idea of all these things being pursued in moderation—the idea of steering a middle course. These common threads, and the difficulties of weaving them into a viable policy, appear to some extent in regional planning exercises recently undertaken in most if not all advanced economies, but a consideration of the experience of Scotland, Ireland and France will suffice to reveal their true nature.

CHAPTER 2

Growth Centres in Practice

IN THE previous chapter we noted the variety of interpretations placed upon the growth-centre concept, by authors concerned primarily with theoretical developments. Despite this inexactitude, or perhaps because of it, explicit attempts to devise and implement growth-centre policies have been legion, and are rapidly increasing in number (Rodwin, 1970; Kuklinski, 1972). By "growth-centre policies" we mean those policies designed to bring about a greater degree of intra-regional spatial concentration of economic activity than would otherwise be likely to occur, and to do so by favouring areas of promise rather than areas of need. This definition begs a number of questions and does so necessarily because, as the following discussion shows, these policies vary considerably in both conception and design. But they are united by a common thread which, though slender, is both real and, in contrast to earlier regional planning practice, revolutionary—the notion of positive spatial discrimination as a tool of regional development.

The present chapter focuses upon three countries—Scotland, Ireland and France—which for a decade have pursued regional policies with a clear growth-centre element, albeit with differing emphasis and varying consistency. Clearly, other advanced countries—Italy, Norway or Poland, for example—might equally have been selected for study, but it is contended that the policies pursued in Scotland, Ireland and France are sufficiently varied to highlight many of the underlying assumptions and issues involved, and it is with the validity of these assumptions and issues that this book is primarily concerned.

SCOTLAND

McCrone (1969) has noted that although certain earlier government reports advocated explicit policies of spatial discrimination in promoting development in Scotland, notably Scottish Council (1952), it was the Toothill Report (Scottish Council, 1961) which first effectively demanded emphasis to be shifted away from shoring up areas of decline, as indicated by unemployment levels, towards stimulating areas of promise. The prime concern of the Toothill Committee was the slow rate of growth of the Scottish economy: unemployment, emigration and other problems were subsidiary to this. And so, "the essence of the plan is quite simply the simultaneous removal of the factors which restricted growth and the encouragement of those which will promote it" (p. 186). The spatial elements of the plan flowed from this statement.

Particular emphasis was placed upon ensuring an adequate supply of labour for the new industry which it was hoped to attract, and so on providing housing in chosen locations for displaced workers from areas of decline. Special transfer allowances were recommended to facilitate the movement of the unemployed to these chosen areas. Without identifying the latter, the report made it clear that the four Scottish new towns already established in the Central Lowlands should number among them. In effect, the Toothill Report heralded a shift of emphasis in new-town policy away from providing for "overspill" towards providing the spatial framework for a policy of accelerated economic growth. The latter was to be promoted not just by the benefits of adequate pools of labour, but by the advantages of concentrating public investment in restricted areas and by the various external economies which newly established firms bestow upon their neighbours. A shift in emphasis, then, from accommodating growth to stimulating it, and from areas in need to areas with potential.

The *Central Scotland* White Paper of 1963 (Scottish Development Department, 1963) accepted both the primacy of the growth objective and the importance of growth areas in achieving it. "Experience has shown . . . that this is the best way to coordinate effort and spending so that economic growth can take place on the right scale and with speed." To attack the deficiency of sufficient and suitable labour for new firms it set out policies for promoting retraining and labour mobility—the latter by accelerating housebuilding programmes in the growth areas, by establishing a "resettlement transfer scheme" to facilitate the movement of redundant workers and by offering financial help to new growth area firms to defray journey to work expenditure. And while the growth areas could not be offered preferential rates of financial aid for new industry, they were, in contrast to the usual policy of supporting development districts only through times of high unemployment, assured that in their case the normal fiscal and financial inducements would be continued until there was "strong evidence of a general and sustained improvement in employment in Central Scotland as a whole" (p. 32). Accordingly, the growth areas have enjoyed at least development district (or "area") status ever since, making them, according to Johnston *et al.* (1971), *primi inter pares* (p. 324).

The White Paper was none too clear on just how the eight growth areas were selected (Fig. 2.1), though it spoke of looking at prospects for growth

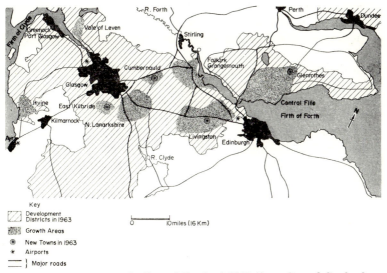

Key
- Development Districts in 1963
- Growth Areas
- New Towns in 1963
- Airports
- Major roads

0   10miles (16 Km)

Fig. 2.1. Growth areas in Central Scotland 1963 (from *Central Scotland: a Programme for Development and Growth,* Cmnd 2188, by permission of HMSO).

and the potential for attracting ample labour resources. Four (now five) contained designated new towns and so were obvious choices. The others contained a petro-chemical complex (Grangemouth/Falkirk), a number of major industrial estates plus the Ravenscraig steel strip mill (North

Lanarkshire) and a good deal of concentrated American investment (Vale of Leven). (Another interpretation is that first selected were those areas outside Glasgow and Edinburgh with the greatest growth potential as indicated by new town status, location and past performance, with certain "rehabilitation areas" such as Fife, West Lothian and North Lanarkshire, where unemployment and dereliction were pronounced, being tacked on later.) Certainly it seems that by designating growth *areas* rather than centres and by nominating as many as eight in a region no more than 80 miles by 30, some concession was made to the political forces which always favour the short-term advantages of dispersal. And it is likely that there were similar motives behind the statement that "indeed, by forming focal points of especially vigorous economic development, particular growth areas will help to create a favourable climate of growth in the wider catchment areas associated with them". Such an objective, promoting development away from the chosen areas, was clearly very much subsidiary to that of maximising the growth of the Scottish economy as a whole.

Another White Paper followed less than a year later (Scottish Office, 1964), reaffirming the policy of spatial discrimination, reviewing the industrial and infrastructural prospects and progress of each of the eight areas, and noting that about half of the year's new industrial building in Central Scotland had taken place there. But thereafter rather less explicit attention was paid to the favoured role of the growth areas in government pronouncements. The plan for the Scottish Economy from 1965 to 1970 (Scottish Office, 1966) continued the theme of integrating policies of overspill and of industrial estates in order to provide stimuli for economic growth, but it spoke (p. 57) of opening up *new* areas of development after 1968, citing three in particular. And, according to McCrone (1969), the spatial pattern of investment in Central Scotland in the mid/late-1960s was by no means as concentrated in the eight growth areas as earlier reports had anticipated.

Nevertheless, for at least two of the growth areas, the Lothians and Grangemouth/Falkirk, detailed plans for stimulating and accommodating the proposed growth were drawn up (Scottish Development Department, 1966 and 1968a). There, and in the various new towns, the administrative machinery exists to promote the desired economic growth (Scottish Development Department, 1970b, and annually).

Although no comprehensive review of the success of the eight growth areas in attaining the goals set out in 1963 and 1964 has yet been published, it is clear that the new towns at least have been strikingly successful in attracting new industry, and in achieving the rapid growth intended (Cresswell and Thomas, 1972; Taylor, 1973). More significant, the Scottish new towns do seem now to be viewed more as foci and generators of growth than as mere overspill reception centres. "Central Scotland . . . demonstrates more clearly than elsewhere the evolution of the relationship between new towns and regional planning and, in fact, displays this relationship in its most advanced form in Britain" (Diamond, 1972, p. 61).

Central Scotland, containing 75% of the country's population and 90% of its manufacturing industry, naturally warrants close attention, but the very sparsity of population and industry elsewhere makes the rest of Scotland equally interesting in a consideration of growth-centre policies. Common features of much of Scotland north and south of the central lowlands include a declining workforce in primary production (especially in agriculture), stagnation in traditional industries such as textiles and agricultural processing, depopulation, the shrinking of small towns and villages and increasing difficulty in the provision of public services. In the context of these problems, a variety of policies have been devised in recent years which, in their explicit or implicit acceptance of the desirability of spatial discrimination, may be considered as growth-centre policies.

In the plan for the Scottish Economy from 1965 to 1970 (Scottish Office 1966) particular concern was expressed for the *Borders*, where rapid depopulation was threatening the adequacy of the provision of both public and private services and, because of its effect on the size and skills of the labour force, the possibility of attracting new industry. In the hope of arresting the vicious circles of depopulation and economic stagnation, a case was made for building up Berwick-upon-Tweed (population 12,000), the main town in the east, and Galashiels, a centrally located town also with about 12,000 inhabitants and with a further 60,000 people living within a 15-mile radius (Fig. 2.2).

Immediate, if necessarily modest, steps were proposed to build up industry and population in Galashiels, but consultants were commissioned to consider in more detail the relative merits of Galashiels and its neighbouring towns in a longer term programme of expansion. In the context of our study of the objectives and interpretation of growth-centre policies,

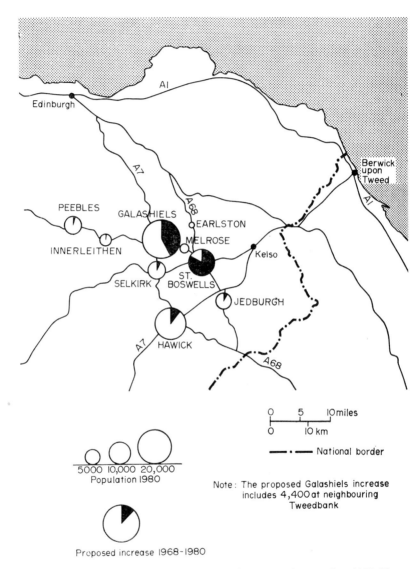

FIG. 2.2. The Central Borders: proposed pattern of expansion 1968–80 (after *Central Borders: a Plan for Expansion*, by permission of HMSO).

it is significant to note that in proposing growth at Berwick and Galashiels the government was aiming first at stimulating more lasting economic growth, and second at making possible the continued provision of high order services. The consultants' task was to *allocate* a *given* target of population and economic activity in and around Galashiels in an area termed the Central Borders, and their eventual proposals constituted primarily an attempt to minimise *per capita* expenditure on social and economic infrastructure—a third objective of growth-centre policies (Scottish Development Department, 1968b).

The consultants were required to produce a strategy for an area of about 400 square miles, containing about 75,000 people and seven towns with a population between 2000 and 20,000. Their allocation of the "given" 25,000 expansion by 1980 between these and other settlements was based on the notion of building a "regional city": "all development should aim towards the concept of a regional community, with facilities and amenities comparable with those of a city" (Scottish Development Department, 1968b, p. 7). Industrial estates were located with reference primarily to labour supply and service provision, but residential location depended chiefly upon a consideration of the marginal costs to the public sector of expansion in each town, using "urban threshold analysis" (discussed below, in Chapter 4). The subsequent annual reports of the Scottish Development Department indicated a broad measure of local authority agreement with the consultants' proposals and a determination to implement them. But there has been pressure to reduce the high growth target for the centrally located village of St. Boswells, and to channel more growth to the existing centres (Warren, 1972).

In the *Highlands* of Scotland regional planning has since the mid-1960s been effectively in the hands of the Highlands and Islands Development Board, set up in 1965 to promote the economic and social development of that region. Although normal town and country planning matters rest with the local authorities, and although the Board lacks effective control over the pattern of infrastructure, the latter is able to offer a wide range of incentives, including ready-built factories, to promote economic growth in the region and to fashion a spatial strategy that it feels most appropriate for that purpose. In designing that strategy the Board has had to take account of the sparse and scattered distribution of population (280,000 people in 14,000 square miles), widespread depopulation, high unemployment, very low activity rates and only about 10% of the workforce being engaged in manufacturing. It was immediately faced with the difficulty of pursuing both equity and efficiency—of neglecting neither the needs of the tiny scattered settlements of the west and the islands (where "the clearances" remain a sensitive issue), nor the obvious growth potential of the Moray Firth area around the regional capital, Inverness. It decided to designate three "major growth areas" suitable for large-scale manufacturing industry and substantial increases in population, plus a number of "small industrial growth points" in the west and the islands. (Any development elsewhere in the region would be in rural activities—forestry, agriculture, fishing, tourism and recreation.) In effect, a threefold categorisation of industrial centres appears to be in operation: first, the inner Moray Firth; second, Wick/Thurso and Fort William, each with an initial industrial endowment; third, the various small growth points (Fig. 2.3).

The Moray Firth, a strategically placed lowland with deep-water estuaries, clearly has a crucial role. Its population of about 70,000 is about one-quarter of the region's total. Its favoured status as the prime growth area is justified by the Board in terms of its potential for providing services and employment for virtually the whole region, and by the inescapable fact that the expressed objectives of promoting the economic growth of the region as a whole and of restructuring the region's economy to one based more on manufacturing activity *must* require that it backs its only real winner (HIDB, 1968). Figure 2.3, based on maps in the Board's report for 1971 (HIDB, 1972), shows that of the industrial sites in the region which have been selected by the Board for assistance where possible, and of the factories and workshops built by the Board or with the Board's money, about one-half are in the inner Moray Firth area. A flexible sub-regional strategy was prepared by consultants (Holmes, 1968), indicating how the area might accommodate any population up to 300,000, and by means of a vigorous programme of industrial promotion, the Board has been able to supplement the recently established aluminium reduction works at Invergordon with a wide range of light industry.

More recently, the exploitation of North Sea oil and gas has given a new stimulus to the development of the Moray Firth area (Milligan, 1973). Oil-related developments, notably a major fabrication plant, various engineering services and material supply depots, are being established in the area and are likely to bring 5000–7000 jobs by 1975 (HIDB, 1973).

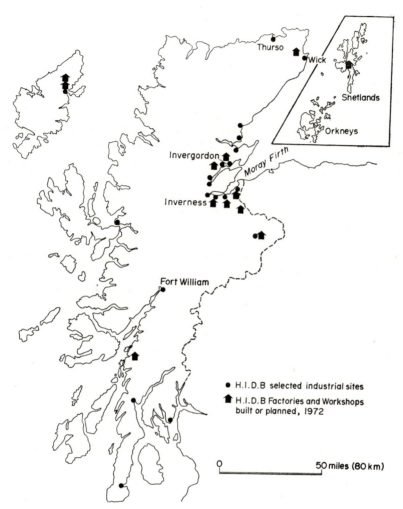

Fig. 2.3. The Highlands and Islands Development Board—Factories and Industrial Sites (from *Sixth Annual Report* (*1972*), Highlands and Islands Development Board, courtesy of HIDB).

The second-tier growth centres seem certain to experience less dramatic growth. The Fort William urban area, now with about 12,000 inhabitants, has shown steady industrial expansion and diversification since the establishment there in 1966 of a large pulp and paper mill. Wick and Thurso, in the extreme north, seem less well placed to build on the growth enjoyed in the 1960s following the establishment by the Atomic Energy Authority of an experimental reactor and associated plants. Only very modest success in attracting new employment was made in 1972 (HIDB, 1973).

Regarding the third tier, twenty-five centres of population have been identified (Grieve, 1972) where services and labour are encouraged to concentrate—partly to stimulate primary activities and tourism, but partly in the hope of attracting a small amount of manufacturing activity as well. Some success, though very modest, has been achieved: a single firm employing a dozen local people can, of course, make a great deal of difference to an isolated community with a few hundred inhabitants. Nevertheless, the general impression obtained from the Board's literature is that these third-tier centres can expect little or no growth outside the primary and tourist sectors, though every encouragement will be given to any entrepreneur who may wish to locate there. Growth has certainly not been channelled to the west, though it has sometimes taken place there.

At the time of writing (mid-1973), the Board is reassessing its spatial strategy, and major changes may be forthcoming. The scale of the oil-related developments in the Moray Firth area appear to indicate that private sources of finance may be sufficient to develop the area as fast as labour supply and other constraints allow. In this case, the Board may feel free to divert its attention and its largesse elsewhere. In short, it is faced with the classic growth-centre dilemmas of whether, when and to what extent growth should be diverted from the area with greatest promise.

Of the other Scottish regions, a growth-centre policy has been prepared for the *North-east*. In that region, the consultants (Gaskin *et al.*, 1969) argued that the first priority was to consolidate the total population by the mid-1970s, that this could only be achieved by an influx of 8000 new jobs, largely in manufacturing industry, and that in turn the best way of achieving this was by channelling public investment to two growth areas, the Aberdeen city region and, to a lesser extent, an area around Elgin. Again, unforeseen oil-related developments have forced a reappraisal of the strategy. There is little difficulty for Aberdeen in achieving its target, as it has quickly become the principal servicing base in Scotland for North Sea oil and gas exploitation. But Elgin has much less growth potential, compared with Peterhead 60 miles east, which has already grown considerably because of its suitability as a servicing base (Milligan, 1973). In any event, the strength of rivalry between Elgin and neighbouring towns of similar size appeared likely to prevent full implementation of the Gaskin proposals, even without the oil and gas bonanza.

The *South-west* is the only major region of Scotland for which a regional strategy was devised, at least in large part, by representatives of the local authorities, rather than by central government or by consultants. It may be in consequence of this that its main recommendations relate to the manner of attracting industry, not to its location (Scottish Development Department, 1970a). No explicit selection between urban centres was made.

Three broad conclusions may be drawn from this review of growth-centre policies, as practised in Scotland. First, they demonstrate a wide range of objectives. Foremost among these is the promotion of economic growth, especially by attracting new manufacturing industry. Other objectives, generally of secondary importance but varying in emphasis between regions, include an improvement in the provision of services and amenities and of the net ability of the region's inhabitants to make use of them, a minimisation of the marginal *per capita* costs of public investment and a reduction of outmigration by the stimulation of employment and service facilities in the most attractive places. Second, the designated growth centres differ greatly in form, size, areal extent and composition. Third, the policies reveal the considerable difficulties of pursuing long-term strategies of deliberate discrimination. Not only can the plans be overtaken by unforeseen technological developments, notably in this case the exploitation of new energy resources, but they are highly susceptible to the exigencies of local democracy and pressure-groups. It is this latter factor which largely accounts for any wavering away from original resolutions—a tendency apparent, though to different degrees, in each of the regions reviewed.

IRELAND

Of the two Irish states, it is *Northern Ireland* whose experience more closely resembles that of Central Scotland. The Belfast Regional Plan (Matthew, 1964) was concerned mainly with the physical problems of the growth of Belfast and proposed a new regional centre (Craigavon) and nine "centres of development" which in size and function closely resembled the overspill towns of Central Scotland. The Plan also advocated the expansion of six "key centres" elsewhere in the province in order to stem migration into Belfast. This proliferation of centres for growth was criticised in the Wilson report (Wilson, 1965) which, like the 1963 Central Scotland White Paper, reassessed the physical structure of the region in terms of its potential for generating economic growth. Efforts were subsequently made to concentrate a large part of residential and industrial development in just four new towns, Craigavon, Antrim, Ballymena and Londonderry (Fig. 2.4). Two of these, Craigavon and Ballymena, have a clear overspill and migrant interception role, but the prime objective of this policy has been to create the most favourable conditions for industrial attraction and expansion (Boal, 1973).

The 1970–5 Northern Ireland Development Programme (Matthew *et al.*, 1970) explicitly favours a growth-centre policy, primarily in order to ensure sufficient concentration of labour and of services to attract new industry to the province, but also to help achieve the more local problems of redeveloping Belfast and of stimulating new employment in the west. But on the face of it, the programme does appear susceptible to the familiar criticism of having chosen too many centres to be fully effective. First it argues that care should be taken not to hold back Belfast to the extent that firms needing a big city location are deterred from coming to the province. Then it proposes that most of the rest of the growth should take place in seven "centres of accelerated industrial growth", namely the four new towns and three other towns close to Belfast. But in addition it identifies eight "key centres", which would be not just centres of service provision, but made positively attractive to new industry. That makes fifteen centres in all, plus Belfast.

While Northern Ireland displays marked spatial disparities in rates of growth, with Belfast and the east growing twice as fast as the counties west of Lough Neagh, the *Irish Republic* may be said to constitute a classic example of centre–periphery dualism—which typically accompanies progression from an agrarian to an industrial economy (O'Neill, 1971). Dublin, with 26% of the population and 40% of net output, dominates the space-economy and O'Neill noted the clear tendency for Dublin to increase its proportion of the nation's manufacturing industry in the 40 years to 1966. Indeed, analysis of the 1971 census figures (Parker, 1972) suggests that despite the policies reviewed below, the gap is still widening.

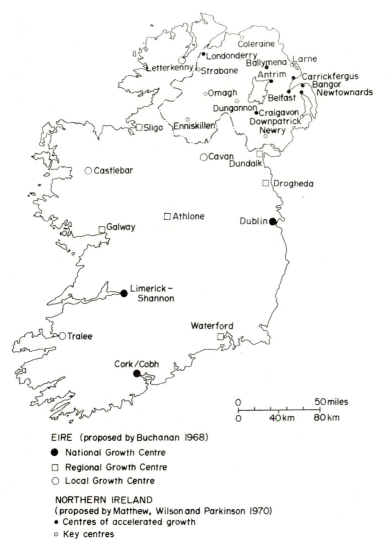

EIRE (proposed by Buchanan 1968)
- ● National Growth Centre
- □ Regional Growth Centre
- ○ Local Growth Centre

NORTHERN IRELAND
(proposed by Matthew, Wilson and Parkinson 1970)
- • Centres of accelerated growth
- ○ Key centres

FIG. 2.4. Growth centres proposed in Ireland (after Buchanan (1968) and Matthew *et al.* (1970)).

Although the flow of migrants to Dublin is apparently being stemmed, between 1966 and 1971 60% of the nation's population increase still took place there and it is now a city of 850,000 inhabitants. In absolute terms, its growth was more than double that of all the other national and regional growth centres put together (see below).

With spatial disparities widening between Dublin and the rest of the country, increasing concern has been expressed about the depopulation of the rural counties, deterioration in the level of service provision and the rapid destruction of the rural character of Irish life, for example by Newman (1967). But the real dilemma in which Irish planners have been placed derives from the apparent incompatibility of these *regional* goals with certain of those for the *nation* as a whole. The latter have been set out in a number of planning documents (e.g. Eire, 1964; Eire, 1969) and include an increase in the overall rate of economic growth, an increase in real *per capita* incomes and a reduction in the emigration of many of Ireland's most able people—a problem which has beset the country for over 100 years. The central problem of Irish regional planning is how to reconcile these goals, which appear to require a spatial structure geared primarily to economic growth, with those relating to regional "balance" and the preservation of rural life.

It was in the early 1960s that regional planning really began to look for a solution. In the 1950s attempts had been made to foster the establishment of small-scale industries in the rural west, under the 1952 Underdeveloped Areas Act. The most ambitious project was the construction of the Shannon Industrial Estate, intended both to provide employment in a problem area and to help revitalise an airport threatened with being by-passed by modern jet aircraft. By 1967 the Estate employed over 3000 workers (Kupper, 1969). But, as in the UK, the middle and late 1950s were generally a period in which the whole nation's interests were put first (O'Neill, 1971).

In 1963 the Second Programme for Economic Expansion (for the period 1964–70) placed greatest emphasis on industrial expansion, but declared that the establishment of "centres of economic and social growth" would assist in this. Then, in 1965, the Report of the Committee on Development Centres and Industrial Estates came out clearly in favour of a growth-centre policy in industrial development—not to promote inter-regional industrial movement (as in Scotland, for example), but "to secure a substantial increase in the volume of industry in the country as a whole by creating the necessary environment for this purpose" (Newman, 1967, p. 25). However, while the Committee was careful not to "take sides" in the argument of how few or how many, the National Industrial and Economic Council was quick to suggest that "in a country the size of Ireland there can be only a limited number of such centres—perhaps in the foreseeable future not more than six outside Dublin and Cork" (NIEC, 1965, quoted by Newman, 1967, p. 26), a policy reaffirmed in its later pronouncements (NIEC, 1968, 1969). The government's reply was explicitly in favour of the development-centre concept as a way of promoting national growth and of bringing industry to the regions, but apart from saying that a start would be made by designating Galway and Waterford as growth centres, the government decided to await comprehensive regional surveys before going any further.

Two such surveys, for the Dublin and Limerick regions, had been commissioned in 1964, primarily to provide advice on the compatibility and co-ordination of local plans in the context of national economic objectives. The "Advisory Plan and Report for the Dublin Region" (Wright, 1967) made the assumption that Dublin's share of the nation's population would remain constant and accordingly apportioned the national growth target, derived from the Second Programme. This implied an increase of 300,000 by 1985, and although most of this would inevitably be located with 10–15 miles of the centre of Dublin, Wright did propose in addition four "development centres" further afield, those at Drogheda and Newbridge being scheduled for major expansion. Thus, the rationale of Wright's "development centres" lay in their overspill and migrant interception roles.

The "Report and Outline Plan for the Limerick Region" (Lichfield, 1967) was intended to advise on "the general size, form and function of the urban settlements within the region . . . with particular reference to centres of potential for economic and social growth" (p. 5). It too worked from the basis of national economic objectives, and included an implicit local objective—the "conservation of the pattern of community life". In deciding where to locate the predicted growth of population and industry, three alternatives were considered: concentrating all industrial development in the central growth axis of Limerick–Ennis–Shannon, dispersing it to most settlements of any size (as proposed by the Limerick Rural Survey, cited by Newman, 1967), or steering a middle course. Evaluation was attempted using the "planning balance sheet" variant of cost–benefit analysis and the mid-way course was selected. Nevertheless, this meant that nearly two-thirds of the predicted population increase of 64,000 by 1981 would be located in Limerick and Shannon, although a number of smaller centres were promised limited growth and small industrial estates or sites. The plan also proposed a policy of "selected settlements" (large villages and small towns) for the concentration of population and services in "retarded areas". Thus Lichfield's growth-centre policy rested partly on ensuring the conditions for industrial expansion, but also on attempting to make available to most of the region's inhabitants the possibility of benefiting *in situ* from an improvement in employment and social opportunities.

Following on the heels of the regional strategies for Dublin and Limerick, as promised in the government's pronouncements in 1965 concerning the need for a national spatial strategy based on the growth-centre idea, the document *Regional Studies in Ireland* was published in 1968 and is probably the nearest thing to a comprehensive national spatial strategy that any of our three case-study countries have produced (Buchanan and Partners, 1968). Its national extent, and its articulation of various interpretations of the growth-centre concept, make it worthy of close study.

The consultants' brief was to examine in detail the seven regions presently without regional strategies, but to take account of those prepared for the Dublin and Limerick regions. Their terms of reference were to "indicate growth potential, identify possible development centres, establish the level of change needed in infrastructure to facilitate growth and make proposals for policy decisions to be taken by government, including measures to implement such proposals" (p. i). As they interpreted it, "the essence of the regional planning problem is to answer the question: which pattern of urban settlement or combination of patterns will best meet the economic and social aims of the Second Programme?" (p. 12) and they identified what was termed "the key question": "if it turns out that the requirements of economic growth and industrial efficiency . . . and the social aims of rural development policy . . . are in conflict, how shall their conflicting claims be reconciled?"

Central to their work was an analysis of the development potential of every Irish town with more than 5000 inhabitants (except the three largest, Dublin, Cork and Limerick), using a wide range of economic and social criteria which related both to the towns' roles as regional centres and to their suitability for industrial expansion. Then, five alternative strategies were developed, ranging from one of maximum concentration around Dublin to one of extreme dispersal of industrial activity. These were evaluated in terms of the nation's objectives, particularly those relating to reducing emigration, unemployment and rural depopulation, and to promoting rapid industrial expansion. The best balance of advantages lay with a strategy incorporating elements drawn from the above five.

Four tiers of urban centres were identified for suitable promotion (Fig. 2.4). First, the three largest cities, termed "national growth centres", would perform the role of providing the basis for industrial expansion. Of these Dublin was deemed to have sufficient momentum to make most appropriate a policy of merely catering for growth as it occurred. But Cork and Limerick would require special assistance if they were to reach 1986 population targets of 250,000 and 175,000 respectively—equivalent to a doubling of the population of Cork and a tripling of that of Limerick. Second, six "regional growth centres", presently with 10,000 to 30,000 inhabitants, were recommended for growth to targets between 18,000 to 55,000. Each was intended to enjoy some industrial growth, though to a varying degree, and emphasis would be placed particularly on their role as major regional service centres. (Of the nine planning regions, seven would have one national or regional centre, the North-east would have two, and Donegal none.) Third, a number of "local growth centres" were proposed (four initially, with perhaps others later) for areas well away from the main centres, to serve as a focus for the concentration of regional services and of such industry as might move to their vicinity. Finally, Buchanan recommended a "village growth-centre" policy for the rationalisation of the distribution of population and services in remote rural districts—though without identifying specific places. Overall, the consultants judged that compared with a possible policy of greater concentration their proposed strategy would be somewhat less successful in promoting economic growth and stemming emigration but more successful in achieving regional balance, curtailing rural depopulation and preserving rural traditions. It was a skilful and, indeed, persuasive compromise, but its reception was mixed.

The National Industrial Economic Council (1969) quickly came out in support of the Buchanan proposals: "The choice is not, therefore, between two paths towards full employment by 1980—one concentrating on building up a few major centres and the other offering all or most towns and villages the immediate prospect of the same rate of expansion. This is a choice between the possibility of full employment in 10 or 15 years' time and full employment, if at all, in some indefinite and very distant future. This is the background against which the Buchanan Report must be considered" (p. 7). And it observed that "the Buchanan strategy . . . is not . . . a strategy for apportioning the economic growth that will in any case occur . . . it is a strategy which will accelerate growth . . ." (pp. 10–11). O'Neill (1971) went further and criticised Buchanan for not proposing *sufficient* concentration. She suggested a strategy with only five growth centres in the whole of Ireland—Dublin, Belfast, Cork, Galway and Londonderry.

But the government was clearly less enthusiastic for different reasons. In the Third Programme 1969–72 (Eire, 1969) it reaffirmed the arguments for growth centres and set out a résumé of the Buchanan proposals—but it did not explicitly endorse them. Then, in 1972, a government agency charged with encouraging industrial growth in Ireland, the Industrial Development Authority (IDA) produced a set of regional industrial plans which differed substantially from the Buchanan proposals (Eire Industrial Development Authority, 1972; *Irish Banking Review*, 1972; Parker, 1973). The IDA set itself a target of providing 55,000 more manufacturing jobs in the Republic by 1977, but claimed that Buchanan had been too pessimistic about the prospects of achieving such a goal without heavy emphasis on the promotion of major growth centres. Whereas Buchanan proposed that 75% of industrial expansion should take place in his nine regional and national growth centres, the IDA proposed a figure of only 50% and argued that Dublin should grow only at the rate of its own natural population increase. Particular attention is to be paid to the regions west of the Shannon, and to towns in the 3000 to 16,000 range which, on the basis largely of a recent examination of industrial movement in Ireland (Ohuiginn, 1972), are said to have considerable growth potential. It is hardly surprising that the proposals have been criticised (Parker, 1973) as too "dispersionist" to achieve their own growth targets.

So, at the time of writing, the Irish pendulum seems to have swung back away from concentration towards greater dispersal—but it is too soon to say how permanent this movement is likely to be. Suffice it to say that the whole debate neatly illustrates the dilemma which is at the heart of regional planning in Ireland. In the Limerick study, Lichfield expressed it in terms of resource utilisation. "Constantly our thinking is forced back to one question: granted that Ireland has only limited resources, should they be invested in trying to raise the level in the less developed . . . areas, or in pushing ahead in the developed areas as fast as possible so as to create new wealth from which the aid to the poorer areas can come?" (Lichfield, 1967, p. 23). The author of the Dublin regional plan, Myles Wright, highlighted the restricted scope of possible government action and stressed its limited ability to swim against the tide of increasing population concentration: "They can encourage moves in the desired direction by exhortation and—within strict limits—by financial inducements. More they cannot do. The average Irishman . . . will vote with his feet or cheque book directly the bargain looks much less than fair. These potent factors . . . underlay the major proposals of the Dublin regional plan" (Wright, quoted in Viney, 1969, pp. 18–19). But, of course, while Wright could anticipate that feet and cheque books would "vote" in favour of his Dublin-based strategy, a good deal of ballot-box voting may go the other way, and the strength of political opposition to any policy which smacks of accepting increased rural depopulation and the demise of Gaelic traditions is *itself* one aspect of reality with which the planner must contend. This political argument and the related fact that Ireland's planning process is "indicative rather than prescriptive" (Black and Simpson, 1968, p. 28) will seemingly always tug the position of compromise back from the concentration end of the spectrum.

FRANCE

In a review of growth-centre policy in France, Bernard (1970) defined his subject as "coherent efforts to stimulate the development of certain priority localities in the hope of providing a greater stimulus to the general development of a particular area" (p. 64). He identified two kinds of growth centre in France—industrial complexes, both large and small, and higher-order urban centres where the emphasis was placed upon their tertiary function. The latter interpretation is more original in conception and execution and, in a comprehensive review of the subject such as this, it deserves more attention. But French regional policy, like policy in Britain, evolved from a phase of almost exclusive attention to the manufacturing sector, which we examine first.

As in Ireland, concern has frequently been expressed in France about the wide disparities between the capital city and the rest of the country, whether measured in terms of income, unemployment, net migration or industrial structure. And since at least 1955 attempts have been made to rectify this by a policy of industrial decentralisation (Allen and MacLennan, 1970). The year 1955 saw a battery of measures introduced to control development in the Paris region, to promote the decentralisation of government, to provide the finance for regional expansion and, most interesting from our viewpoint, to establish twenty-six "critical zones" for particular assistance in the task of attracting new industry. These zones, like the British development districts of the early 1960s, were based almost exclusively upon measures of unemployment and the notion of rescuing areas in distress. But they did introduce the notion of spatial discrimination, even if in future relatively more attention was to be paid to potential rather than to need.

In the Third Plan (1958–61) and, more particularly, the Fourth Plan (1962–5) the emphasis shifted from the relief of congestion in Paris and the rescuing of problem areas towards the notion of each region playing a positive role in meeting national objectives—particularly that of rapid economic growth. The idea of *entraînement* was introduced, i.e. of stimulating growth in chosen areas by the judicious deployment of public investment (e.g. in Bas-Rhône–Languedoc) and in 1964 the scattered "critical zones" were replaced by vast areas where varying degrees of assistance were promised to firms moving out to France outside the Paris region (Fig. 2.5). But the most favoured area, which covered much of western France, did contain eight urban areas (shown black on the map) for especially generous assistance and several of these, e.g. Brest, Lorient, Nantes, Bordeaux and Toulouse, were large towns with a considerable endowment of public infrastructure and external economies. Spatial discrimination continued but the emphasis was shifting to growth potential.

One other kind of *industrial* growth centre described by Bernard is the integrated industrial complex developed in part with public funds. A fairly modest example is the National Telecommunications Study Centre which, together with associated electronic factories, employs about 2000 people at Lannion in northern Brittany (Bertrand and Dubois, 1970). Much larger are both the industrial complex of the Golfe de Fos on the Mediterranean coast, which has been variously forecast to employ between 80,000

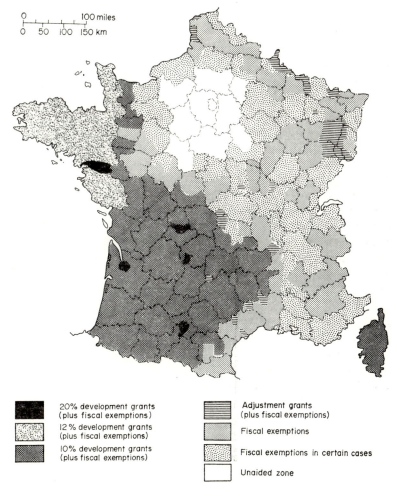

FIG. 2.5. France: aid for regional industrial expansion 1966 (courtesy of the French Embassy Press and Information Service).

and 200,000 by 1985, and the petro-chemical complex at Lacq in the Pyrenees. The total regional impact of the latter has been described as both slight (Penouil, 1969) and considerable (Bernard, 1970). The essential idea of such interpretations of growth centres is nevertheless one of cumulative growth by means of internalising links within the complex.

Since the mid-1960s, however, there has been a shift of emphasis in French regional policy from the manufacturing to the tertiary sector and from industrial complexes to urban centres. This stemmed partly from an appreciation of the growing dominance of the tertiary sector in employment terms (36% in 1954, 38% in 1962, 45% in 1968) and the diminishing ability of purely industrial location policies to rectify regional disparities, and partly from the evidence provided by the 1962 census regarding the process of urbanisation (Urbanisme, 1965). The census confirmed the very rapid growth of towns with over 100,000 inhabitants and the inevitability of continuing urbanisation as a concomitant of economic development—particularly as with "only" 67% of its population in urban centres, France had at that time a long way to go to reach the levels of nearer 80% in the UK, the USA and West Germany (Piatier, 1965). It also revealed that despite the particularly rapid growth of medium-sized cities, the gap between Paris and the next largest cities was widening. The ratio between the size of Paris and that of the second city had increased from 5 to 1 in 1800 to 8 to 1 in 1962. Planners decried the top heavy urban hierarchy and drew invidious comparisons with the much less centralised spatial structures of Germany and Italy (Antoine and Weill, 1965; Hautreux *et al.*, 1963; Hautreux, 1966). Particular attention was drawn to the disparity between the size–distribution of French cities and the "norm" set out in Zipf's law: when the logarithm of the population of each city was plotted against that of its rank, it was clear that in contrast to the good fit described by medium-sized towns, Paris was well above the "ideal" diagonal line and the next nine towns (from Lyon to Strasbourg) were well below it (Fig. 2.6). This "irregularity" was afforded great significance, although a graph of conurbations (Fig. 2.7) was less deviant and despite there being no *prima facie* reason why such an urban size–distribution should be inimical to the main concern of the Fifth Plan, namely economic growth.

Parallel to this concern with the inevitability of considerable further urbanisation and the apparent unsuitability of the existing urban network to accommodate it were feelings of dissatisfaction on two other fronts. First, there was a feeling that most French citizens should be able to enjoy a range of social, administrative and cultural facilities which were presently available only to those with access to Paris (Bauchet, 1961). Second, and

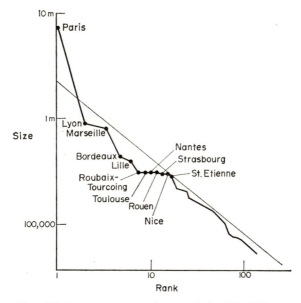

Fig. 2.6. French towns: rank–size relationship 1962.

this was forcibly expressed in the Fifth Plan (Commissariat Général du Plan, 1966), there was considerable concern for the productivity of French industry in an increasingly competitive international climate. In spatial terms, this implied that such industry as was to be diverted to the under-developed west and ill-structured east should be carefully channelled to the most promising locations there, the major cities. And in hierarchical terms, it suggested diversion away from "congested" Paris to those centres offering the best basis for self-sustaining growth by dint of their labour supply, service provision, existing industrial base, etc. Allen and MacLennan (1970) have written that this approach is "in marked contrast to recent British approaches to regional development which have stressed the benefits accruing from a fuller utilisation of underdeveloped resources in the poorer regions. There is, of course, something of this in the French planners' view, but their main concern is that regional development will help increase, or at the very least not hinder the rate of growth of *productivity*" (p. 178).

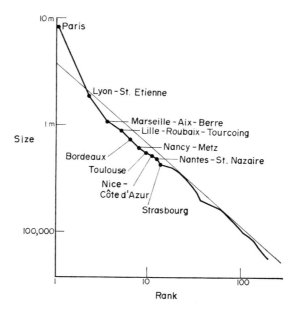

FIG. 2.7. French conurbations (zones de peuplement industriel et urbain):
rank–size relationship.

These various elements, the appreciation of rapid and inevitable urbanisation, "excessive" concentration of population and services in Paris, the cultural barrenness of the provinces and the need to promote and protect increases in productivity, generated a concerted attempt to restructure the French urban system, and a determination to place immediate emphasis upon the upper echelon of the hierarchy. Thus was born the policy by which a few of the largest provincial cities were deliberately selected with the intention of there "simulating the external economies and metropolitan functions of Paris" (Allen and MacLennan, p. 305), so that both consumers and industry would reduce their dependence upon Paris. Their function was to "balance" the pull of Paris and, accordingly, they were termed *métropoles d'équilibre.*

The procedure used for selecting these cities has been set out by some of the researchers involved (Hautreux, 1966; Antoine and Weill, 1965; Hautreux *et al.*, 1963; Documentation Française, 1969) and accounts in

English are given in Hansen (1968) and Allen and MacLennan (1970). Reference was made, in apparent ascending order of significance, to the size of the available labour forces, to the cities' external influence as indicated by business linkage, railway and telephone communications and migratory flows, and to their central place function. On the latter point particular attention was paid to the incidence of high order and rare services—commercial, cultural, educational, administrative and professional. Eventually eight cities were chosen which were very largely those below the diagonal line in Fig. 2.6, except that Rouen was excluded because of its proximity to Paris, and Nancy and Metz were included as a single Lorraine *métropole* (Fig. 2.8). Membership of the top tier was to be strictly limited to eight, to increase their chances of success, but similar criteria were used to identify ten "regional centres" whose function was rather loosely described as "relaying the influence" of the *métropoles* within their regions. And attempts were made to identify further towns in lower tiers of the hierarchy, where infrastructure might be concentrated for the benefit of the rural inhabitants—partly, no doubt, to allay fears of excessive favouritism towards the *métropoles*.

The *métropole d'équilibre* policy was written into the Fifth Plan (1966–70). It was to be pursued in a number of ways. First, the *métropoles* would be given priority in programmes of public investment in higher education, cultural amenities, hospitals, administration—and in other sorts of public overhead capital appropriate to their superior hierarchical level. And, according to Hansen (1968), the regionalisation of the 1966 budget did incorporate some positive discrimination in their favour. Second, efforts would be made to decentralise to them such public and quasi-public organisations which did not require a Paris location, including certain government research establishments. Third (DATAR, 1971), measures were introduced in 1967 to subsidise between 5% and 20% of any investment by the private sector which resulted in at least fifty research and development or 100 administrative jobs being transferred from Paris to the *métropoles* or to certain other major regional centres—about twenty towns in all. And, finally, government assistance was promised for a programme of comprehensive "structure planning" exercises for each *métropole*, by setting up *organisations d'études d'aménagement d'aires métropolitaines*.

The *métropole d'équilibre* policy has since been subjected to a number

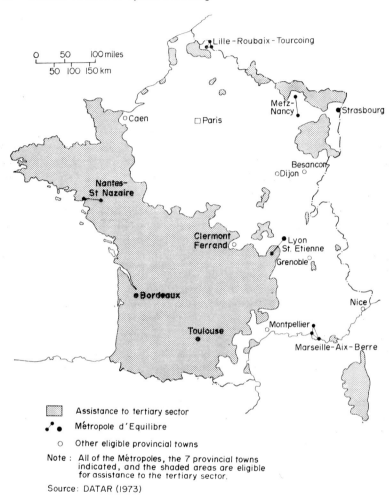

Fig. 2.8. France: assistance to the tertiary sector.

of criticisms. First, the selection was based on measures of past performance, not an explicit appraisal of growth potential. Second, fragmentary evidence of possible diseconomies of further growth in the larger *métropoles*, of the rapidity of growth of rather smaller towns—in the 100,000 to 200,000 range (Lewin, 1965)—of a certain popular preference for life in towns in that size range (Hansen, 1968) may suggest that on opportunity cost grounds attention might have been better concentrated lower in the hierarchy. Third, advocates of this latter policy have also expressed fears that the *métropoles* will drain their regions of population and investment, just as Paris has done at the national scale. There is little empirical (or, indeed, theoretical) basis for the belief that *métropoles* will stimulate development in areas 100 miles or more away, and the role of the various intermediate centres in the hierarchy has never been made clear. Fourth, if the object is to provide the best possible milieu for an effective growth of production and of productivity, then it may be unwise to ignore the claims of large towns which have undoubted growth potential but which are "too near" to Paris: Rouen is the prime example, others are Dijon and Orleans. Such towns would appear to combine the best of all worlds from an industrialist's point of view, as well as having an equally deserving case for advanced service provision from the viewpoint of the resident. Finally, there are inevitably doubts about the degree to which any democratically elected government can effectively pursue such a selective policy in the distribution of its largesse. Allen and MacLennan (1970, p. 218) noted that "the industrial development of the less prosperous regions of France is being encouraged by the very definite and by no means arbitrary selection of areas where the growth of population and employment could most feasibly take place and the creation in advance in these locations of the external economies which are considered to be the major influence on costs and therefore the location decision". But Bernard doubts the effectiveness of these good intentions: "There has been no lack of statements affirming the existence of an official policy concerning the rational organisation of space around a hierarchy of centres . . . yet . . . in the case of the *métropoles d'équilibre*, there appears to be an extraordinary slackness about the action taken in pursuit of that policy" (1970, p. 96).

Recent developments suggest an increasing degree of vigour in the policy of decentralising the tertiary sector from Paris, but an apparent reduction in the priority afforded to the *métropoles*. In January 1972 more effective measures were introduced to control office development in Paris, and financial incentives for firms moving service jobs to the provinces were stepped up (DATAR, 1973). The new investment grants are 20% for administrative and managerial employment creation, 15% research and development, and 20% if the registered office of the company is transferred from Paris. But the places eligible for such assistance have been radically changed. The *métropoles d'équilibre* and the select handful of other major regional centres have now lost their élite status. The new investment grants are payable to suitable firms which move either to these major cities or to any part of an extensive portion of France outside the Paris region. The areas for assistance to the manufacturing and tertiary sectors are now identical (Fig. 2.8). Evidence for 1972 suggests that these measures have succeeded in accelerating decentralisation and that in practice most firms in the tertiary sector do move to provincial towns with over 100,000 inhabitants. But the *métropoles* have received only thirteen of the twenty-nine major financial establishments which have recently moved from Paris and an even smaller proportion of the major cultural activities which have been established in the provinces since 1966 (DATAR, 1973).

Although it is difficult and somewhat premature to attempt a firm conclusion about the effectiveness of growth-centre policies in France, there does seem to have been a clear tendency for places to be designated some form of preferential status, but without practical policy ensuing. And yet it seems reasonable to agree with Bernard's conclusion (Bernard, 1970) that the growth-centre concept has provided a "guiding principle", however diffuse, for the past decade of French regional policy—a guiding principle which warns of the costs of policies of scatter and extols the benefits to be reaped from judicious policies of grouping related activities together.

CONCLUSION

It is contended that the major issues revealed by a consideration of growth-centre policies in Scotland, Ireland and France are, in fact, universal. They emerge equally in relation to the United States (Hansen, 1970), Canada (Higgins, 1972), Italy (Allen and MacLennan, 1970), Spain (Richardson, 1971), Poland (Regulski, 1972) and in any other country where positive spatial discrimination is deliberately practised as a tool of regional planning. The basic issues are first, how far is concentration necessary upon economic grounds, and how might the economic optimum be reconciled with the very real political and social forces which generally press for greater dispersal? Second, even if an approximate solution might be found to this at the theoretical level, how should specific centres be selected and subsequently promoted? These are difficult questions which call for a much better understanding of the need for careful goal specification and of the decision-making process—points of policy taken up in the concluding chapter.

But some progress ought to come also from a more thorough understanding of the degree to which growth centres might reasonably be expected to fulfil the various roles which are ascribed to them—and it is to this theoretical issue that the remainder of this book is devoted. For it is clear that not only do growth centres, as tools of planning policy, vary greatly in size, form and composition, but they also embody a wide range of objectives held dear by the policy-maker. First they have been conceived as providing the most conducive spatial framework for the attainment of rapid economic growth—and so we shall need to examine the nature of agglomeration economies and their relevance to the process of growth (Chapter 5). Second, growth centres have been promoted as an economically efficient means of service provision—in terms both of the capital expenditure to which the public sector is committed when growth occurs and of the private and public costs of effectively providing services for a static or declining population. Chapter 4 is therefore devoted to the economics of service provision and to the relevance of urban size in this context. Third, growth centres have been seen as compatible with, and possibly even conducive to, an objective of raising levels of development throughout an extensive problem region, not just in the few favoured locations where investment is first concentrated. The propensity of growth centres to stimulate development in the regions within which they are located is the subject of Chapter 6. A fourth objective relates to the effect of growth centres upon migration—do they effectively intercept migrants who would otherwise be bound for overcrowded metropolises, and do they make their region more attractive to key personnel from other regions? This is the subject of Chapter 7. Finally, an objective may be discerned which relates to the acceleration of the diffusion of innovations into backward regions and of the stimulus to development that innovation adoption brings. The promotion of growth centres in this context has been more frequently explicit in developing countries (e.g. Misra on India (1972) and Friedmann on Venezuela (1966)), but, as the next chapter argues, this may simply reflect a degree of ignorance among planners in advanced economies about the process and importance of innovation diffusion, and perhaps a misguided belief that the adoption of innovations is not affected by the urban strategy which they choose to pursue.

CHAPTER 3

Urban Centres and the Diffusion of Innovations

THE concept of "development", unlike that of "growth", relates not simply to a process of quantitative expansion, but to one of qualitative change. Thus, economic and social development is concerned with fundamental transformations within an economy or a society. It involves the spread and acceptance of new ideas and new ways of doing things: in short, it is inextricably tied up with the diffusion and adoption of innovations. "Development . . . is an innovative process leading to the structural transformation of social systems" (Friedmann, 1969, p. 4). "The process of development . . . can be conveniently described as the introduction and diffusion of successive waves of innovations in functional . . . and in geographic space" (Hermansen, 1972b, p. 6). We have already noted (Chapter 1) the key role attributed by growth-pole theorists to the ability of leading firms and industries to affect development within a system of linked industries by means of their power to innovate. Here, in our consideration of growth-centre theory, we are concerned with the nature of regional development and the possible role in its promotion of the diffusion of innovations via urban centres. If it is true that "self-sustained economic development in a region cannot take place without the continued adoption of innovations in the region, (and that) policies for regional economic development will to a large extent be policies for the inducement of innovation diffusion" (Pedersen, 1971, p. 137), then to what extent should the promotion of growth centres play a role in such policies?

One justification for growth-centre policies is that innovations are necessary for development, that innovations are normally introduced in successively lower levels of the urban hierarchy, but that in many cases, "instead of development 'trickling down' the urban size-rachet and spreading its effects outwards within urban fields, growth is concentrated in a few large urban centres and a wide gulf between metropolis and countryside is apparent" (Berry, 1969, p. 189). Such a "blockage" in the process of innovation diffusion is best dealt with by means of a judicious programme of expanding chosen centres in key locations and at key points in the urban hierarchy. Thus it is argued that "the role played by growth centres in regional development is a particular case of the general process of innovation diffusion" (Berry, 1972, p. 108). And so, in this chapter we examine the theory of the spatial diffusion of innovations and consider whether growth-centre policies might be expected to accelerate the process of innovation diffusion in lagging areas and, hence, of regional development. The crucial issue is that of urban size—is it true that the larger the major town of a backward region, the sooner and more effectively it is likely to adopt innovations?

"INNOVATION" AND "DIFFUSION"

The essence of "innovation" (unlike "invention") is implementation. "Innovation is the successful introduction of ideas perceived as new, into a given social system" (Friedmann, 1969, p. 9). Note that the idea need only be *perceived* as new—often it will be borrowed or imitated. And note also that the term is not restricted to "the practical application of technical knowledge in production, but also (to) the replacement of old forms, traditions and ways of doing things . . . the introduction of new specialities in production and consumption, the emergence of new industries, new types of social and industrial organisations, etc." (Hermansen, 1972b, p. 7). Examples of innovations which are relevant to development and which have been studied in their spatial dimension include street railways (Krim, 1967), television stations (Berry, 1972), fluoridation of water supplies (Crain, 1966), planned shopping centres (Cohen, 1972) and city-manager-style governments (McVoy, 1940)—as well as technical developments in manufacturing industry (Pred, 1966). The *diffusion* of innovations concerns simply "the acceptance over time of some specific idea or practice by individuals, groups or other adopting units" (Katz, Leven and Hamilton —quoted by Berry, 1972, p. 108). Hence, the *spatial* diffusion of innovations is concerned with the acceptance of innovations in both time and geographical space. It is with the role of urban centres in such diffusion that we are concerned.

But first we must draw a fundamental distinction between "household" and "entrepreneurial" innovations, the former having immediate effects only on the adopter (usually a person or family), the latter having direct consequences for people other than the adopter, who may be a person, a firm, a city, etc. An example of the former is the installation of running water in a dwelling; of the latter, the installation of a water-supply system. Further, as the adoption of a certain entrepreneurial innovation often precludes its successive adoption in the same town, then, in effect, it is the town which does the adopting, and so "we might therefore call entrepreneurial innovation, urban innovation" (Pedersen, 1971, p. 38). It is *this* kind of innovation that interests us in the transmission of regional development impulses via the urban system—but, unfortunately, much of the literature on the spatial diffusion of innovations has been concerned with the localised spread of household (and agricultural) innovations, e.g. Hagerstrand (1952, 1967).

Parallel to this distinction between "household" and "entrepreneurial" innovations is a distinction between two kinds of spatial diffusion—"neighbourhood" and "hierarchical". It was the former, with its emphasis on the overriding importance of physical distance in the diffusion process, that was emphasised by Hagerstrand and other students of household innovations. The distinction has been expressed by Cohen as follows: "The neighbourhood effect means that . . . the closer a potential adoption unit to the source of innovation or to another unit that has already adopted . . . the greater the probability that it will adopt. . . . The hierarchical effect implies that . . . the higher the ranking of a potential adoption unit in a hierarchy, the greater the chance that it will adopt . . ." (Cohen, 1972, pp. 14–15). This two-fold categorisation has been extended by Brown (1972), who considers innovation diffusion at the macro-, meso- and micro-scales, relating respectively to diffusion within an urban system, within the hinterland of a single urban centre and within a small area or single community. But the point is simply that in initiating a process of regional development, it is a "hierarchical" or "macro" model that is of most interest, because this illustrates the "short circuiting" of the neighbourhood diffusion process and because it appears much more applicable to the more basically important entrepreneurial innovations. And so in this chapter (cf. Chapter 6) we are concerned primarily with the *first* of the two diffusion processes observed by Berry in the United States: "The developmental role of growth centres involves the simultaneous filtering of the innovations that bring growth down the urban hierarchy and the spreading of the benefits accruing from the resulting growth . . . from centres . . . to . . . periphery" (Berry, 1972, p. 108).

THE ROLE OF URBAN SIZE IN INNOVATION DIFFUSION

(a) *Empirical Evidence*

Entrepreneurial innovations typically originate in the very largest cities. Analyses of the location of patents awarded in America in the late nineteenth century (Pred, 1966) and of the introduction of a wide range of innovations into nineteenth- and twentieth-century Chile (Pedersen, 1970) affirm that this is so. Indeed, Lasuen (1973) goes further and claims that today most innovations in the western world originate in four megalopolises: the eastern and western American seaboards, the Ruhr–Rhine valleys and the London–Midland plain. But what is important to this discussion is the role of urban size not in the *generation* of innovations (since it would be pointless to expect backward regions to solve their problems by developing a major metropolis), but in their subsequent *adoption* elsewhere.

Certainly, in the latter half of the nineteenth century the adoption of entrepreneurial innovations was closely tied to the urban hierarchy. A study of the timing of the installation of street railways in American towns (Krim, 1967) shows a clear relationship between date and population size (Fig. 3.1). Also instructive in this context is a study by Pyle (1969) of the diffusion of cholera in nineteenth-century America. In the early part of the century, the disease clearly spread spatially, with distance from the origin being the prime factor. In 1866, however, city-size was most important: the epidemic entered in the big ports, especially New York, and a graph of the logarithm of city size against date of arrival (May to December 1866) reveals a very similar relationship to the one discovered by Krim.

Finally, Pedersen's work (1970) on the adoption in Chile of fire-brigades, hospitals, waterworks, radio stations, etc., in the late nineteenth and early twentieth centuries confirmed a significant, if relatively weak, relationship between date of adoption and size of town. Pedersen attached greater

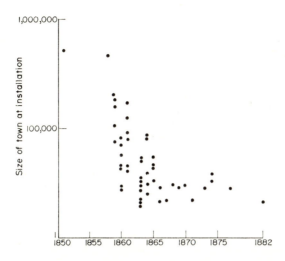

Fig. 3.1. Diffusion of street railway adoptions down the American urban hierarchy, 1851–80 (from Krim (1967) in Perloff (ed.), *The Quality of the Urban Environment* (1969), by permission of Resources for the Future).

importance to the fact that 70–85% of the adoptions occurred in towns after a *near* larger neighbour had adopted, i.e. some combination of the hierarchical and neighbourhood effects was at work.

Studies of the diffusion of more recent innovations confirm the importance of urban size. Berry (1972) considered the timing of the opening of television stations in US cities between 1940 and 1968. A very clear relationship $(r^2 = 0.60)$ emerged between the logarithm of the population of the town and the year of opening (Fig. 3.2). Population "potential", a measure of the aggregate accessibility of each town, added little to the explanation. A study of "planned regional shopping centres" (essentially out-of-town centres which in size and range of goods and services resemble a central business district) reveals a similar pattern (Cohen, 1972). Between 1949 and 1968, 151 American cities adopted this innovation and 40% of the variance in the date of adoption was attributable to measures of urban size—population, disposable income, level of retail sales, etc.

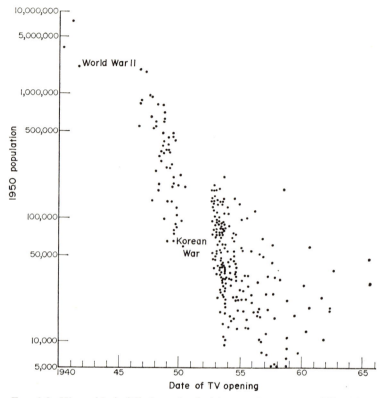

FIG. 3.2. Hierarchical diffusion of television stations among US cities (after Berry (1972) in Hansen (ed.), *Growth Centers in Regional Economic Development*, by permission of Macmillan, NY).

(b) *Possible Explanations*

Why should entrepreneurial innovations tend to be adopted by progressively smaller towns? There are a number of possible explanations.

(i) *Information flow.* In much of the pioneer work on the spatial diffusion of innovations (notably by Hagerstrand, 1952, 1965, 1967), the role of information availability was afforded paramount importance. Thus, in Hagerstrand's simulation model of the diffusion of agricultural innovations in Sweden in the 1930s, the adoption of an innovation by farmers in any given locality was held to be dependent primarily upon the likelihood of their receiving information about it—itself very largely a function of distance from a previous adopter. Later modification, e.g. the introduction of distortions due to barriers to communication such as forests and marshes, and attempts to simulate *resistance* to change by requiring potential adopters to receive the information several times before acting, did not destroy the essence of the model and the overriding importance attached to information receipt.

Even in concentrating on information receipt, however, Hagerstrand was less than comprehensive. He considered only inter-personal communication, not the mass media; he virtually ignored the interpretation of information and the complex process of learning and decision-making (Hermansen, 1972b); and his conception of distance was wholly geographical, not social (Pred, 1967). And yet Hagerstrand may fairly claim that his simulation models "worked"—in the sense that their output bore remarkable resemblance to the pattern of real world innovation diffusions with which he was concerned. What is at issue, however, is whether this emphasis on information flows may be transferred from household to entrepreneurial innovations, from neighbourhood to hierarchical diffusion and indeed, from the 1930s to the 1970s.

When he turned his attention to entrepreneurial/hierarchical diffusion, "Hagerstrand, who views diffusion of innovations as a learning (persuasion) process . . . approached the problem by considering that there exist networks of social communications which connect certain places (central places in this case) to the exclusion of others" (Brown, 1969). In other words, Hagerstrand claimed the existence of a hierarchy of information networks, local, regional and international, by means of which innovations are transmitted (Fig. 3.3). Misra (1972) has recently advocated the careful fashioning of a hierarchy of urban centres (which he terms "poles", "centres" and "points") in India, in order primarily to promote the efficient functioning of these information networks and thence the diffusion of innovations to rural regions.

Pedersen (1971) has suggested that the flow of information is likely to accord closely to the gravity model, with the exchange of information between two towns depending upon their size and spacing. And he suggests that in developed (cf. developing) countries, the mass factor is likely to be more important in explaining interaction than is distance between centres.

But no empirical evidence is presented. Information availability *may* still be peaked locally, as it undoubtedly was in the nineteenth century, to which Pred's work (1966) on urban growth relates, but the mass-media and the mushrooming of technical journals have surely led to information flow about entrepreneurial innovations being both more rapid and more widely spread than ever before. And such work that has been done on interpersonal communications (e.g. Brown, 1968, in southern Sweden) fails to confirm the existence of "regional-type" contacts, which might explain "short-circuiting" in the spread of information and give the hypothesised hierarchy of information flows. In short, it is doubtful whether the clear tendency for entrepreneurial innovations to diffuse down an urban hierarchy in an advanced economy—as shown in Fig. 3.2, for example—is primarily attributable to the manner of the diffusion of information about these innovations.

(ii) *Markets.* An alternative explanation of the role of cities, and of large cities, in the adoption of innovations revolves around the need to minimise risk. The introduction of a new process or product is inherently a risky business for its propagator and, as Pred noted (1966, p. 99), "uncertainty has a spatial dimension". Problems of a technical nature may arise, or of factor supply (particularly labour and capital) or of marketing, and each is likely to be more easily overcome in (large) cities. The argument is not simply that technical expertise, skilled labour and a ready market are most abundant in cities, but also that relevant information about them, and therefore the ease of solving any problems that arise, is greater. Thus, in one sense, the argument here too is one of abundance of information, but not specifically about the innovation, rather about the requisites of their adoption. We consider markets first.

The idea is that the most profitable (or least risky) locations are exploited first, and successively less profitable or more risky locations are exploited later—hence time of adoption will vary with size of the untapped market. This statement need not apply only to the private sector, although Brown and Cox (1971) contend that it is particularly appropriate when the propagator is self-interested. In the public sector, too, timing may depend on the intensity of effective demand, on the scale of problems resistant to solution by traditional means (Friedmann, 1969), and so, perhaps substituting "urgency" for "profitability" in the above discussion, we have a possible explanation for the early adoption by big cities of such innovations as city-manager-style government (McVoy, 1940), fluoridation (Crain, 1966) and fire-brigades (Pedersen, 1970).

Thus, "an entrepreneurial innovation can in many cases only be adopted when a number of households are ready to adopt the corresponding household innovation" (Pedersen, 1971, p. 38). And for private-sector innovation it becomes important to understand the distribution policies of the propagator of the innovation and the shopping trip behaviour of the potential adopter. With this in mind, it may seem hardly surprising that the diffusion of entrepreneurial innovations should closely follow the central place hierarchy, as the latter is *based* on marketing considerations (Brown, 1969). (This brings us to the question of "thresholds", or of "support populations" whether viewed as potential buyers or as supporters of an organisation. This subject is taken up in greater detail in Chapter 4.)

Finally, it must be noted that what is important is strictly not the absolute size of the market, but the propagator's *perception* of its potential profitability. Thus factors other than the strictly economic may arise, including the degree to which individual urban markets are known to the entrepreneur. This knowledge might vary directly with proximity to the home of the entrepreneur, so again information availability is seen to be relevant—not information about the innovation, but about the nature of potential markets.

(iii) *Factors of production.* The argument here is broadly similar, i.e. that labour, capital and entrepreneurial skill are in short supply and are most readily available in the largest cities and thereafter in progressively smaller places.

Thompson (1965) has stressed that the adoption of innovations requires flexible and diverse *labour*, research-oriented technical manpower and imaginative management, and it is clear that the absolute number of people ready, willing and able to perform a certain job of work is clearly likely to vary closely with size of urban centre. This is subject to the usual *ceteris paribus* reservations, of course, since large one-industry towns would be less attractive in this respect. The subsequent diffusion of innovations down the urban hierarchy from the largest cities might be explicable by pressure on wage rates and by difficulties of recruitment, brought about by the building up of demand for the specific requisite skills in the major

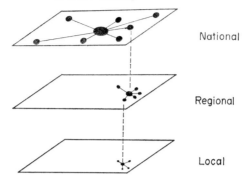

National

Regional

Local

FIG. 3.3. Diffusion through the urban hierarchy.

centres. *Capital*, it is true, tends to be much more mobile at least within the national frontiers of developed economies, although Richardson (1973a) suggests that inter-regional capital flows largely follow the urban hierarchy. In any case, money-lending institutions will themselves be concerned with the "geography of uncertainty" and so look unfavourably on many proposed small-town projects and, where public funds are concerned, there may, of course, be absolute deficiencies of capital if the local tax-base is small. Finally, if the location of people with *entrepreneurial* talents is largely random, as Pedersen (1971) suggests, then the probability of at least one entrepreneur being present in a town will be largely a function of its size. In fact, the personal and commercial attractions of big cities for such people probably results in their being more than proportionally represented there, thus strengthening the argument. Diffusion down the hierarchy in this case may stem less from the exhaustion of entrepreneurial talent in the big cities than from an "imitation process", whereby small-town entrepreneurs mimic the actions of those in larger cities (Berry, 1972).

(iv) *Social factors.* "An alternative . . . argument is one couched in terms of the differential resistance of urban places of differing size; larger places adopt first because they are more cosmopolitan and less resistant to innovation" (Brown and Cox, 1971, p. 559). Indeed, of the six factors which Friedmann (1969) lists to explain the spatial pattern of innovation adoption in his *General Theory of Polarized Development*, three are essentially social: he refers to a place's "capacity for absorption of innovation, without undergoing major structural change", the "frequency of innovative personality traits" and the "social rewards offered for innovative activity". (His other three factors relate to information, scale of demand and availability of resources: each has been discussed above.)

A place's "capacity for absorption" may depend in part on the rigidity of its social structure, and Pred has cited the class-divided social systems of small southern cities as a factor inhibiting their growth (Pred, 1966). Furthermore, large cities may have so many agencies concerned with promoting change that they effectively institutionalise their capacity for absorbing innovations. In addition, Brown (1968) has stressed the "degree to which an individual's orientation is external to a particular social system"—an attribute which he terms "cosmopoliteness" (Brown, 1968, p. 19). The incidence of this, too, is likely to vary with urban size, with many of the more educated members of society who take part in extra-local activities clustering in the larger cities. Such people may not only be more receptive to new ideas themselves, but also act as "opinion leaders" breaking down the barriers of resistance provided by other citizens of the town—a role stressed by Gould and Tornqvist (1971).

SOME CAVEATS ABOUT URBAN SIZE

But while there is no lack of evidence to confirm a general tendency for entrepreneurial innovations to move down the urban hierarchy, nor of possible explanations to account for it, it would be wrong to attach too much weight to this. Other factors influence the diffusion process.

(a) *Urban Location*

It is not clear that the overall relationship between size and timing of adoption holds true *throughout* the urban hierarchy. Visual inspection of the graphs relating to television stations in the mid twentieth century (Fig. 3.2) and to street railways in the late nineteenth century (Fig. 3.1) suggests that below a certain size (perhaps around 50,000 inhabitants) the relationship is far from clear. This accords with the study of the adoption of planned regional shopping centres in the United States which found that urban size was virtually insignificant in the latest stages of the diffusion. After 1963, or *very* roughly below 200,000 inhabitants, the chronology of adoption was much harder to explain (Cohen, 1972). Studies specifically of innovation diffusion among very small towns confirm this. Brown (1968) found that the adoption of liquid propane gas tanks in one county of Wisconsin occurred significantly earlier in urban rather than rural areas— but that the actual size of the urban areas was insignificant (all had fewer than 7000 inhabitants). And Hudson (1969) found that the timing of the adoption in North Dakota of such community innovations as nursing homes and swimming pools could be explained as much by the spacing of the urban centres as by their hierarchical rank.

This is fragmentary evidence, but it does suggest that in time hierarchical diffusion tends to break down and give way to other patterns. Probably the *location* of urban centres becomes more important. The neighbourhood effect, apparently crucial in the diffusion of many household innovations, clearly emerges in several studies of entrepreneurial innovations also. Thus Crain (1966) found a clear tendency for those American municipal governments which were early adopters of fluoridation to influence their undecided neighbours. It would be interesting to try to establish how typical is the tendency for entrepreneurial innovations to spread first hierarchically and then areally, and what determines the point at which a changeover occurs. Clearly, this would have important ramifications for growth-centre policies promoted in order to accelerate the introduction of innovations into a lagging region.

In areal or neighbourhood diffusion there are two scales to be considered—one heartland/hinterland (or intra-national), the other urban centre/nodal region (or intra-regional). Berry, for example, has referred to the "simultaneous filtering of innovations . . . down the urban hierarchy and the spreading of benefits . . . both nationally from core to hinterland regions and within these regions from . . . centres . . . to . . . periphery" (Berry, 1972, p. 108).

Regarding the intra-regional type of neighbourhood diffusion, the point is that "a low order place (will) adopt sooner than other low order places if it is near a previous adopter" (Brown and Cox, 1971, p. 554), or, as Hudson graphically put it (1969, p. 52), "in terms of diffusion, a town of 1,500 persons 50 miles from New York is in a much different position than an identical size town located 50 miles from Havre, Montana". Thus, the concept of "diffusion down the hierarchy" may have a spatial connotation quite absent in studies which use the expression purely in terms of urban size (viz. Figs. 3.1 and 3.2 above).

This intra-regional type of diffusion is generally explained in terms of the effect of distance on *information* transmission. On the one hand, potential adopters of, for example, a city-manager type of local government (McVoy, 1940) are stimulated by the experience of their neighbours; on the other hand, successful entrepreneurs in the metropolis, intent on expanding their activities, will tend to be better informed of the possibilities presented by nearby towns. Of course, a need for easy access between potential agency and parent body for a wide range of servicing and supervisory reasons would reinforce this "neighbourhood effect".

(b) *Urban Growth*

A number of writers indicate that rapidly growing towns are more likely to adopt innovations than are more stagnant towns of similar size and similar location. Friedmann (1969, p. 12) concluded "historically, conditions especially favourable to innovation are generally present in large and rapidly growing urban systems". And Krim (1967) noted that rapidity of growth was a significant additional factor in explaining the timing of street railway installations in late-nineteenth-century America.

An amalgam of factors already discussed is probably responsible for this. To begin with, it seems reasonable to suppose that rapidly growing towns are likely to be more "cosmopolite" in the sense described above, and hence more receptive to new ideas. And the prospect of a larger market in the near future may induce an apparently premature adoption of an entrepreneurial innovation. Indeed, as the adoption of innovations itself promotes growth of employment and, hence, of population, demonstrated empirically by Berry (1972, p. 134), the process of crossing thresholds may become cumulative. "Once implementation (of inventions and ideas) has occurred, that is once new factories have been erected or old ones enlarged, employment and population increase, the web of interpersonal communications is again extended and densened, the chances for invention, innovation are further enhanced and the circular process continues, perhaps even at an accelerated pace . . ." (Pred, 1966, p. 28). And we need not, like Pred, restrict the concept to manufacturing innovations: this cumulative process may be of much more general and fundamental importance. It will form the basis of Chapter 5.

In addition to the *opportunities* provided by rapidly growing towns, there are also their peculiar *needs*. The very rapidity of their growth may produce unprecedented problems, arising, for example, from intensified pressure on amenities and resources, or from the rapid build-up of a culturally heterogeneous population. The solution of these problems may become a matter of great urgency if growth is to continue and this, too, may foster a greater readiness to try something new—particularly in the public sector (Friedmann, 1969).

(c) *The Nature of Modern Industry*

Finally, it may be that geographical space and the diffusion of innovations between towns and within regions is becoming less and less important to modern industry. Much of the evidence quoted above regarding the regular patterns of innovation diffusion is either historical, e.g. Pred's work on manufacturing industry in the nineteenth century, or else related to modern innovations in the service sector, e.g. Berry on TV stations (1972) and Cohen on planned regional shopping centres (1972) where central place considerations may be expected to be paramount. Unfortunately, very little research has been done on the diffusion of new production techniques and processes and of managerial innovations, but it seems that the organisational structure of industry is likely to be more important in this respect than is urban size or spatial proximity. Most large companies have their own substantial research and development departments and are quick to spread innovations throughout their various establishments, irrespective of their location. Indeed, Lasuen (1969, 1973) sees in the multi-product/multi-plant/multi-city form of modern industry the most promising prospect of spreading development impulses into dispersed parts of the country. It may be, then, that many of the more abstract "growth-pole" notions concerning "organisational space" and the need to attract modern innovative industrial establishments have more relevance to regional development than was admitted in the above discussion (Chap. 1).

CONCLUSION: IMPLICATIONS FOR POLICY

Leaving aside the spatial diffusion of innovations within large industrial corporations, about which relatively little is known, it does appear that the early adoption of most entrepreneurial innovations depends largely upon urban size, location and growth rate—probably in that order. The implications for policies of regional development flow from this. If large urban size provides a conducive environment for the adoption of innovations, if regional capitals tend to be most accessible in inter-regional terms, if the experience of smaller towns depends upon the early adoption of innovations by their larger neighbours and if growth adds renewed vigour to the whole process, then on each count a policy of channelling as much development as possible to a region's largest centre(s) seems justified.

In addition, the preceding analysis of the nature of innovation diffusion suggests other possible policy levers. Though we have argued that the weight traditionally attached to the inter-regional transmission of information may be excessive, any measures designed to improve communications with the main "hearths" of innovation should still prove advantageous. A case in point is the recent establishment in Glasgow of a "planning exchange"—a centre designed to foster the flow of research findings to officers and elected members of Scottish planning authorities, and to assist in in-service training. An excessively cautious or conservative social structure might be ameliorated by a suitable educational programme, though this is likely to prove effective only in the long term. The injection of more "cosmopolite" elements in the society might be achieved by attracting a higher educational establishment, for example, or some other organisation employing nationally oriented and "spiralist"(see p. 156 below) members of the middle class. A deficiency of entrepreneurial talent might be attacked by establishing programmes of business training, by generating a higher level of awareness of local opportunities and sources of support (the work of the British "industrial liaison officers" is relevant here), and by a concerted effort to reduce the level of risk and the obstacles involved in starting up a business. For example, low interest loans might be made available with government backing; so too might "nursery units"—small workshops where budding industrialists could test out the commercial viability of their product and their own business acumen.

Regarding the establishment of service activities which require critical support populations, attempts could be made to reduce threshold levels by subsidising their provision until the level of demand becomes sufficient. Where the introduction of a new facility depends upon the policies of national firms or organisations, "planners . . . should concentrate on manipulating the distribution policy of the propagator of the innovation"

(Brown, 1969, p. 209), i.e. on seeking to understand the basis for entre-preneurs' decisions to introduce innovations in one place rather than another with a view to persuading them of the desirable attributes of the place in question. With this last point in mind, Brown (1972, p. 37) argues that we must "view the diffusion system through the eyes of the principal actors" and therefore calls for an expansion of research into the behaviour of the propagators of "macro" or "entrepreneurial" innovations—a type of research which has hitherto been undertaken only at the "micro" or "household" level.

Finally, it must be stressed that all of these policy suggestions, which largely call for considerable selectivity in the intra-regional allocation of effort and investment, are valid only on a *ceteris paribus* basis. In particular, they stem from an implicit assumption that the goal of maximising some measure of the performance of a problem region *as a whole* is paramount. If other goals intrude, particularly those relating to intra-regional equity, then policy measures may need to be rather different. But this considera-tion deserves another chapter (Chap. 6): so, too, does detailed considera-tion of *why* the early acceptance of innovations is so important and of all the thorny questions related to cumulative causation and self-sustaining growth that this chapter has consistently begged (Chap. 5).

CHAPTER 4

Urban Scale and Service Provision

IN THIS chapter we turn to the economics of the provision of services and examine the argument for growth-centre policies which rests on the supposed greater efficiency of provision in larger centres. We include as services both urban "infrastructure"—roads, sewerage, water supply, etc., and personal services, such as retail distribution and educational and health services. The object, as in other chapters, is to examine the degree to which the spatial concentration of investment is desirable in order to achieve a planned objective, in this case the most economic pattern of service provision.

PUBLIC SECTOR SCALE ECONOMIES

The reason for public investment featuring so prominently in the growth-centre literature lies primarily in the belief that the unit costs of providing, maintaining and operating infrastructure *fall* with increasing urban scale—hence, other things being equal, policies of spatial concentration should be more economic than those of dispersal. Such economies of scale might arise either in the construction or in the subsequent operation of the facility. For either reason, a certain level of provision may be more cheaply attained by one large facility than by a number of small ones, which might be considered necessary if the population were widely dispersed.

The validity of the argument for the existence of some economies of scale in the public sector is attested by several writers (e.g. Cameron, 1970;

Richardson, 1972; Stone, 1972), but rather less agreement is apparent on whether, and if so at what point, diseconomies set in—diseconomies of scale due to the onset of otherwise unnecessary expenditure in large towns, e.g. the installation of complex traffic-control systems. And even more controversy surrounds the notion that might appear to follow from the successive onset of scale economies and diseconomies, namely that an "optimum" city size exists towards which urban planners should strive.

A large part of this disagreement stems from the inadequate way in which scale economies and diseconomies have been examined. Typically, scholars have taken a large sample of towns and have tried to establish how *per capita* public expenditure on one or a number of services varies with size of population. A number of such studies have been reviewed by Richardson (1972) and Hirsch (1968). Thus, for example, a study by Lomax (1943) of English county boroughs indicated that *per capita* expenditure appeared to be least in the 100,000–150,000 range, while Clark (1945), making a comparative study of cities in several advanced countries, arrived at the 100,000–200,000 range. Other more recent attempts, e.g. Hirsch (1959), Duncan (1956) and the Royal Commission on Greater London (1960), produced a variety of apparent optimal ranges of size, usually between 50,000 and 1 million inhabitants.

Along somewhat similar lines is some work on the performance of local education authorities in England, carried out by the Local Government Operational Research Unit (1968). A relationship was sought between the expenditure by the local authorities in certain fields, e.g. specialist staff, textbooks, etc., and a number of socio-economic indices relating to the local authority areas, including population size. Generally, either no relationship or a positive relationship with population size was found, indicating greater expenditure per head of population in the larger areas. But regarding such a relationship, the authors made the following statement: "Interpretation of these relationships is a matter of opinion . . . there is, for example, evidence that larger authorities spend disproportionately more than smaller authorities on textbooks for primary schools. It could be argued from this either that smaller authorities are more efficient than larger, or that larger authorities can provide a better service than smaller" (pp. 11–12). This frank admission appears to place in doubt the value of this and similar attempts, mentioned above, to seek a best size for towns or local authorities on the basis of *per capita* expenditure alone. In other words, analysis of *per capita* expenditure is of little use, unless we know just what is being provided for the money. Very large cities, criticised as unduly expensive by the optimum city advocates, may in fact be providing a range and a quality of services for which their residents are happy to pay. And the niggardly expenditure on services by many small towns may belie efficient housekeeping. The problem, then, is one of measuring the "output" of the public sector—the "benefits" of the cost-benefit ratio. Almost certainly, this output varies considerably from place to place, and renders highly questionable the results of the above studies (Hirsch, 1968; Richardson, 1972).

Attempts have, in fact, been made to relate population size not to expenditure but to indices of the quality of service provided. Most interesting in this context is some work on the determinants of the quality of education and of children's services in English counties and county boroughs (Royal Commission on Local Government in England, 1969). In each case, government inspectors of the local authority services were required to rank each authority on scales of one to five relating to various indices of quality of service, e.g. recruitment of specialist staff, use of certain equipment, etc. The finding for education was that "good authorities can be found through all size ranges, but those below an acceptable level are heavily concentrated in the size group up to 200,000" (p. 231). For both education and children's services, a population of about 200,000 roughly marked the size beyond which an acceptable standard seemed assured: overall efficiency in each case appeared to rise up to about 500,000 and then level off (education) or perhaps decline (children's services). However, from an analytical viewpoint, such research appears susceptible to criticism which is the exact converse to that made in the previous paragraph. Then, exclusive attention to costs at the expense of service quality rendered somewhat dubious the adverse conclusions reached regarding large cities: now, exclusive attention to service quality may render a possible disservice to smaller authorities who may have provided good value on their limited resources.

A way of trying to avoid the problems which arise from both service quality and costs varying with scale of provision is to focus on services which are so narrowly defined as effectively to preclude any serious disparities in quality. Hughes (1967), in his work on Scottish burghs, hoped to do this by concentrating on police, health and welfare and cleansing services. More thorough was Gupta's 'and Hutton's work (1968) for the Royal Commission on Local Government in England. They tried to relate the "cost per unit of output" in a number of specific and, hopefully constant services within the broad fields of housing, highways and health, to the size of the respective local authority areas. Their results strongly refuted the hypothesis that a U-shaped cost curve was the norm. Measures of the costs of constructing a managing council housing, for example, suggested that diseconomies of scale set in at a very early stage. Examination of costs per visit by home nurses also suggested diseconomies of scale, while there appeared some evidence of economies of scale in the upkeep of roads. Where U-shaped curves did emerge, the position of their base varied enormously from about 40,000 (housing management) to 950,000 (highway maintenance by county councils). Perhaps even more important was the finding, made possible by the use of multiple-regression analysis, that such factors as population density, average incomes and social class frequently explained a much higher proportion of the variation in the costs of services provision than did population size.

Another approach is to reject empirical analysis of real-world situations and to attempt an "armchair" costing of the provision of hypothetical but predetermined "packages" of public services in a range of different-sized towns. An Italian exercise along these lines (SVIMEZ 1967, reviewed in EFTA, 1968) found a broadly U-shaped *per capita* cost curve, with a minimum point around 20,000–50,000 inhabitants, a gentle increase to about 250,000 and a sharper increase thereafter.

The results of a rather more comprehensive analysis carried out at the National Institute of Economic and Social Research have been recently published by Stone (1973). Stone set out to establish the effect upon the costs of constructing and operating a new town, of variations in size, shape, form (land-use pattern), density, the system of transportation and the phasing of development. The lack of sufficient variation in these respects among existing new towns and the incomplete nature of data on their construction costs led him to attempt instead to build up "model settlements", using a "kit" of residential and other cells. These cells, and the necessary urban facilities that would be required, were costed using data drawn from a variety of sources—trade journals, new town statistics, etc. He paid particular attention to simulating the likely pattern of travel within the settlements and to estimating the consequent road needs and travel costs.

Three sizes of town were considered, with populations of 50,000, 100,000 and 250,000. Various towns of these sizes were modelled, using different assumptions regarding shape, form, density, etc. An important finding was that there was no significant evidence of either economies or diseconomies of scale in this size range in the construction of housing, public utilities, schools or factories. Any economies of scale were clearly exhausted before the 50,000 size was reached. But there were significant diseconomies of scale in the construction of the main road networks. These costs rose, but at a declining rate: typical *per capita* road construction costs were £80 at 50,000, £100 at 100,000, £120 at 250,000. As the cost of the road network accounted for only about 5% of total construction costs (compared with 50% accounted for by residential development and 20% by industrial and commercial development), the total effect of these diseconomies was quite small. But if we add on the costs of travel to work (the one type of operating costs which Stone was able to study closely), then the effect is magnified and the overall increase in resource costs per head in a town of 250,000, compared with one of 50,000, was estimated to be of the order of 5%.

What was also interesting was that some of the other parameters tended to have a greater effect on costs than did size. Population density had a marked impact on housing and therefore on total costs, with both low and high densities proving expensive. Urban shape affected road network and travel costs, with a rectangular settlement emerging as most efficient. And of the various forms examined, those which were highly centralised tended to be more expensive. Stone concluded (p. 253) that "very broadly, the settlement offering the lowest costs both for construction and the journey-to-work would be a small to medium size town, with a compact shape, and with employment areas spread evenly over the town".

And so Stone's work, like the Italian study, clearly refutes the conventional wisdom that economies of scale continue to be reaped until population sizes of several hundred thousand are reached. But, as the author would doubtless admit, such work is still open to the criticism that the residents of larger towns do enjoy additional services which might compensate for the extra costs. In Stone's work higher education and hospital facilities were provided only in the larger towns. Such provision was not responsible for any significant increase in *per capita* costs, but they must be interpreted as improving the quality of life for big-town residents. It certainly seems illusory to seek an "optimum size", in terms of public sector expenditure, at least until a truly adequate way has been found of measuring the benefits arising.

Even then, of course, it would be nonsense to suggest that the excess of benefits over costs would always be maximised at one particular size. "Since we would never expect the optimal position for each and every firm to occur at the same level of output, why should we expect the optimal point in each city to be located at the same population size?" (Richardson, 1972, p. 30). Obviously, the *function* of towns varies enormously, and it would be as wrong to go to the expense of providing hospitals and expensive road networks in every town as it would be to provide them in no town.

What may need to be optimised is the efficiency of the whole urban system, not just one element in it. Richardson (1972) has pointed to the fundamental theoretical conflict between ideas of optimum city size and of an efficient urban hierarchy. And, looking at a single city within that hierarchy, it may be the internal urban systems which need much more attention than its size. Residential density, urban form and the nature of the transportation system appear to be much more relevant to the costs of building and running a town than is sheer size.

To these criticisms of the concept of optimum city size in the context of public service provision can, of course, be added a range of arguments which oppose any notion of an optimum size in a more comprehensive context. So far we have concentrated only on cost curves. Alonso (1970, 1971) and Hoch (1972) rightly demand that attention be paid to product curves also—evidence of rising real incomes with urban size suggests that productivity tends to be greatest in very large towns. Alonso (1970) has argued that given an objective of maximising net national product, the city should be allowed to grow *beyond* the point of minimum average costs to the point where marginal costs equal marginal product, or at least to the point where the excess of marginal product over marginal costs equals the opportunity cost of redirecting investment to another town. He suggests that this point may not occur until a very considerable size has been reached, though once again it would be necessary to consider separately individual industrial and commercial activities.

Finally, what does all this work on the economics of public service provision and on the possibility of optimal city sizes contribute to the growth centre debate? Primarily, it suggests a minimum size, around 30,000–50,000 perhaps, which is necessary if economies of scale are to be reaped in the provision of certain basic public services. Beyond this size, all the evidence suggests that *per capita* costs rise—but so too do benefits. Without previously establishing the role a town has to play and the price that might be acceptable in order to reap the various social and economic benefits associated with large urban size, it is impossible to define a "best size" towards which public policy should strive. However, the fairly *gentle* nature of the increase in costs at least to around 250,000 (beyond that size less is known) does suggest that even fairly modest increases in benefits might justify the extra expenditure. In a perverse way, the most conclusive thing emerging from the work reviewed above is its very inconclusiveness. The apparent absence of enormous cost differences in the range of urban sizes with which we are mainly concerned leaves the way open for paying more attention to the various benefits that different urban sizes might bring (the subject of much of the rest of this book) and to the cost implications of expanding *particular* urban centres—the subject of the next section.

URBAN THRESHOLD ANALYSIS

If the literature on the economics of public service provision appears to offer little that is more useful than an approximate minimum size for the economic provision of a reasonable range of amenities and a clear indication that, in general, costs vary relatively little over a wider range of sizes, then it may be more fruitful to shift attention from towns in general to the circumstances of specific towns which are candidates for expansion, and from the economics of constructing and managing a town as a whole to those of grafting on a certain scale of new development. This is what urban threshold analysis attempts to do. The idea is that the most economic expansion programme is one which steers development to towns, regardless of their size, with spare capacity in their infrastructure. (This is similar to the idea of "economic infilling" (Green, 1971) as a guideline for village planning, rather than the "physical infilling" traditionally practised.)

This word "threshold" needs some explanation. Its essential connotation in the context of urban planning is one of marking some major discontinuity in the progress of expansion. In this book it is used in three distinct contexts. First, it can denote the onset of more rapid or assured, perhaps "self-sustaining", growth (Chap. 5). Second, the term threshold may be applied to a size of support population at which the provision of a new retail outlet or other service becomes viable (as in the final section of the present chapter). Third, as in the present context, the term is applied to crucial stages in the expansion of a town beyond which major new capital expenditure is required if growth is to continue. Thus, urban threshold analysis (UTA), with its emphasis on the indivisibilities in urban expansion programmes, has been developed as a tool for bridging the gap between physical and economic planners, by making the former more aware of the economic possibilities and implications of laying down new development (Kozlowski and Hughes, 1967; Hughes and Kozlowski, 1968; Malisz, 1969; Jackson and Nolan, 1971, 1973).

UTA involves expressing the onset of these thresholds both carto-graphically, in the form of a map indicating land which might be developed with little, considerable or prohibitive new capital expenditure, and graphically, whereby total development costs are charted against increments of population (Fig. 4.1). The potential value of UTA in urban and regional planning and, more particularly, in deciding upon towns to develop as "growth centres" arises in three ways.

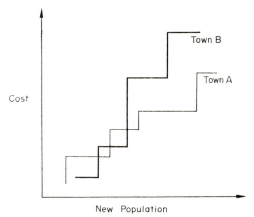

FIG. 4.1. Comparative threshold costs of towns A and B (after Malisz, 1969).

First, it can suggest which single town is likely to require least invest-ment for a given major programme of expansion. Thus, if it were con-sidered desirable for other reasons to concentrate new development exclusively in one town, then the more gently rising generalised cost curve of town A (Fig. 4.1) indicates the advantages of choosing that town. Second, it can suggest how much expansion is desirable in each of a number of towns, if the full benefits of crossing previous thresholds are to be reaped and the costs of crossing new thresholds are to be avoided. Third, a possible programme of development or an "optimal planning path" might be derived in which new development was channelled quickly to a specific town until the next major threshold was reached, and then attention moved to another town—thus avoiding as far as possible the leaving idle of installed capital. Thus, in the regional planning context, the technique does appear to offer one rational way of choosing between centres in terms of their potential for development.

One such application of the technique relates to the selection of suitable settlements for expansion within one of the growth zones previously identified in Central Scotland, namely Grangemouth–Falkirk (see Chap. 2 above). This analysis (Scottish Development Dept., 1968a; Kozlowski, 1968) began with a variant of sieve-map analysis to define land where development was possible without apparently crossing major thresholds, possible but only at the cost of major capital works, or else effectively impossible except at exorbitant cost. This exercise was performed for various types of investment and synthesised to illustrate areas apparently suited for development. Then followed the economic analysis which involved calculating the additional costs involved in locating new inhabitants in each settlement. These costs related to the acquisition and reclamation of land, to public utilities and roads. The product of this exercise is reproduced as Fig. 4.2. It revealed those settlements most suited to large-scale expansion (note the gently sloping generalised curve of Larbert) and formed the basis for suggestions of a sequence of development which would offer the best return on capital expended.

Using a similar approach, the same team of planners and economists attempted to define the relative suitability for expansion of a number of small towns in the "Central Borders" region of southern Scotland (see above, Chap. 2, and Scottish Development Dept., 1968b). Again, for each town they defined public utility thresholds (sewerage and water supply) and physical thresholds, this being an upland area in which topography exerted important constraints. Thence they sought "critical" thresholds, which marked the need for new major services provision, or else the

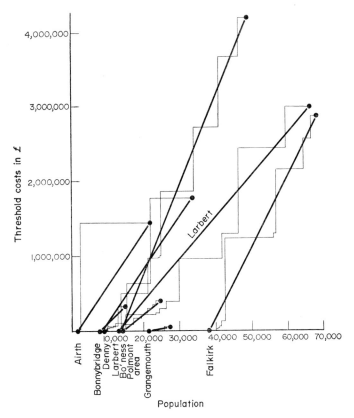

FIG. 4.2. Grangemouth–Falkirk: comparison of threshold costs (from *The Grangemouth/Falkirk Regional Survey and Plan*, Vol. 2, p. 123 (1968), by permission of HMSO).

"ultimate physical limitation" to growth (Fig. 4.3) and it was largely on the basis of this work that a spatial pattern and programme of growth was determined with, for example, St. Boswells being chosen for major expansion (Fig. 2.2).

One further example is provided by a recent examination of the development prospects of a number of small towns in East Anglia (East Anglia Consultative Committee, 1972). In this case attention was focused on

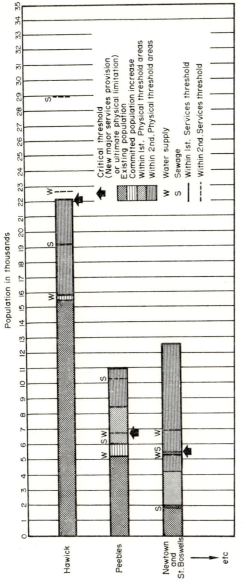

FIG. 4.3. The Central Borders: urban development thresholds (from *Central Borders: a Plan for Expansion*, Vol. 1, p. 13 (1968), by permission of HMSO).

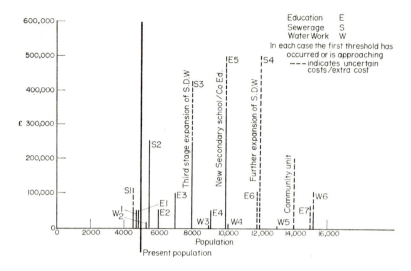

FIG. 4.4. Fakenham: thresholds in public services (from *Small Towns Study* (1972), by permission of the East Anglia Consultative Committee, and the East Anglia Economic Planning Council).

sewerage, water supply and education as three of the most significant services in terms of costs. Figure 4.4 sets out the estimated onset and cost of crossing thresholds in these three sectors for one of the towns, Fakenham. It was partly on the basis of this analysis of thresholds that another contender for expansion, Wisbech, was not recommended as suitable for any significant expansion.

The use of UTA is by no means widespread in British planning practice, although, in theory, it appears applicable in a wider range of planning exercises related to the development of settlements at greatly varying sizes. Jackson and Nolan (1973) have mentioned its use in the planned expansion of the Dorset village of Lytchett Matravers from 1500 to 5500 inhabitants. And if the data could be obtained, some valuable work might be undertaken on much larger proposed schemes than the villages and small towns discussed above.

A number of serious criticisms have, however, been levelled at UTA. Its concern exclusively for the fixed costs of development means that operating costs are virtually ignored. Thus, on the one hand, there is a risk of ignoring low-cost alternative solutions which could allow expansion beyond an apparent threshold, for example, avoiding excessive traffic congestion by staggering journey-to-work times rather than by building new roads. On the other hand, an expansion programme which appears inexpensive in terms of capital costs might produce an urban system which is expensive to operate, for example, because of the costs involved in servicing a remotely located estate by postmen, retail distributors, etc.

A second serious criticism is that UTA seeks a least-cost solution for urban expansion and, in ignoring the potential benefits of different schemes, it marks a retrogressive step compared with cost–benefit analysis (Lean, 1969). This is, of course, a similar criticism to that levelled above at the "optimum city size" advocates who look only at the cost side of the equation. Proponents of the technique have replied that UTA does not preclude more sophisticated appraisals; rather, it might profitably be used as a "budget sieve", narrowing down the field of suitable contenders for such appraisals (Jackson and Nolan, 1971, 1973 review the recent literature on this debate).

Lean has also argued (1969) that in practice the various thresholds, technological, physical and structural, are collectively so numerous and occur so frequently that the onset of any one will largely be offset by the economies accruing from a continuation of expansion beyond a previously crossed threshold. In other words, the rate at which costs rise with increasing scale is, in practice, likely to be fairly constant. This, and the suggestion that thresholds are rarely clear-cut and can often be circumvented by "partial adaptation" in one form or another, may reduce the practical value of the technique.

So UTA may be criticised for fostering an aura of spurious precision. Thresholds may in practice rarely offer such clear-cut choices to the decision-maker—even if they can be accurately defined on the basis of available data, and the assumption of constant technology. And, in focusing only on costs and only on one element of total costs at that, the tool is far from being a panacea in the context of selecting locations for development and for developing growth-centre strategies. But it offers perhaps a more practical way of examining some of the more important public-sector implications of programmes or urban expansion than do notions of optimum size.

THE PROVISION OF PERSONAL SERVICES

We turn now to the changing spatial pattern of the provision of personal services, and to the implications of this for settlement planning. By personal services are meant those which normally require face-to-face contact between the supplier, whether private or public, and the customer. Retail distribution is the obvious example, but the provision of many health, educational, social and entertainment services is also important. The point is, as central place theory has stressed, that such services are market oriented in location, because they cannot usually be stored or transported.

Elsewhere (Chap. 5) we discuss the role of service provision in the fostering of economic growth. The concern there is with what might be termed "producer" services—those required by industry and commerce for their efficient operation. The major role of such service provision in attracting, fostering and stimulating new development is stressed, as is the growing contribution of the service sector to total employment growth. Here, however, we are concerned exclusively with the provision of services for final demand—"consumer" services—and with the welfare aspects of alternative settlement policies.

The reason for this subject being currently of such importance lies in the forces affecting population thresholds, "thresholds" in this context indicating the minimum amount of purchasing power necessary to support the existence of a given service in a given location. A number of economic, social and technological factors are interacting to change the form of the neatly structured hierarchy of service centres postulated by central place theory. Most notable are the pressures for the creation of major new centres near to but not at the heart of our major concentrations of population, and the reduction in the number and importance of small centres in rural regions. It is this latter phenomenon, the declining level of service provision in regions remote from the main urban centres, that concerns us here. What makes this particularly serious is the possibility of a vicious circle of decline: if the service sector is a major source of employment and at least one factor in residential selection, then declining service provision is likely to reduce the scale of demand for other services and so be cumulative. It is important to examine the causes of rising thresholds and declining provision.

(i) *Demand Factors*

The first factor, of course, is the declining size of population in many rural areas. This subject has been much documented elsewhere (e.g. Clout, 1972): suffice it to say that its root cause lies generally in the great improvements that have been made in productivity in the primary sector—agriculture, fishing, forestry and mineral extraction, and in the agglomeration economies which have drawn replacement activities in the secondary and tertiary sectors to the towns. And so, even if population thresholds remained constant, the declining economic base of many rural areas would necessitate some cut-back of the range of services locally available.

Thresholds have not, however, remained constant. Rising real *per capita* incomes have been one factor here. Outlets providing goods and services for which demand is relatively income inelastic—e.g. most staple foods, beer and tobacco—have suffered. A shift in demand towards luxury commodities, e.g. speciality foods and consumer durables, has enhanced the prospects of the larger service centres which specialise in higher-order goods. Concern for greater choice, variety, and range of commodities reinforces this tendency. The result of rising incomes is a widening gap between expectations and the ability of villages and small towns to meet them.

Increasing affluence has, of course, also greatly increased the mobility of all but a small minority of households. Much higher levels of car ownership, more leisure time for travel and major public expenditure on road improvements have certainly increased the ease and speed of travel to larger service centres and have tended to reduce the cost of travel relative to the price of most commodities. This ability to travel greater distances has been reinforced by the ability to store purchased commodities, thanks to the greater living space and to the refrigeration that affluence permits, with the result that long and relatively infrequent shopping trips are replacing short and frequent trips. And, typically, these infrequent trips are "multi-purpose", with previously "low-order" commodities such as groceries being purchased in the same town as consumer durables, etc. Thus, a consequence of greater personal mobility has been further pressure on the viability of village and small town outlets. Greater mobility has had similar consequences in the public sector, with, for example, school bus services drawing widely scattered schoolchildren to larger centrally placed schools.

(ii) *Supply Factors*

Reinforcing the changing nature of the demand for services have been growing economies of scale in their supply. It seems clear that a sharp rise in the cost of labour relative to capital in the retail distribution sector has stimulated a shift to capital intensity, a shift from variable to fixed costs, and the greater indivisibility of capital investment has been a major determinant of larger scale outlets, particularly in the retailing of food.

At the same time there has been a sharp rise in the proportion of the retail market controlled by "multiples"—retail organisations with a large number of branches—for whom centralised buying and the reaping of economies of scale in delivery to their outlets and, where appropriate, from their outlets to their consumers, are more feasible propositions (National Economic Development Office, 1971). And greater price competition, stimulated in Britain by the abolition in 1965 of retail price maintenance, provides further stimulus to the creation of large outlets by making necessary careful attention to the possibility of gaining economies of scale. Economies of scale in the public sector, in the organisation of police and fire services, for example, have had the similar effect of strengthening the relative position of the major towns.

These scale economies have not all been entirely internal to the services concerned. A retailer, considering where to locate a new outlet, will often want to benefit from the drawing power of other stores, whether in a similar or quite different line of business, and so reap the external economies available in a nearby location. So a tendency for *some* outlets to be drawn to major centres is likely to have cumulative effects. In the public sector, increasing emphasis on coordination, on interdepartmental programmes and on central research and intelligence agencies to devise and monitor them, has provided momentum for closing down sub-offices and remote agencies and for clustering more activities around the chief executive and the County Hall computer. Thus interaction, in a variety of guises, works to reinforce the changing character of the demand for services and the growing economies of scale in their supply.

The result of all this has been an attenuation of the urban hierarchy. A marked reduction in the number and importance of the smallest rural service centres is apparent. Hodge (1965), for example, studying the fortunes of service centres in Saskatchewan between 1941 and 1961, noted that variation over that period in the average spacing of centres correlated closely with their rank: small centres had the greatest tendency to die and hence become more widely spaced, and vice versa. Clout (1972) has reviewed a number of studies, e.g. of rural Norfolk, which show similar results in England. This seems a ubiquitous occurrence, not least because a strong cumulative tendency is apparent: growing centres become more accessible and more attractive in terms of what they are able to provide and so are likely to continue to grow—at least to the point where congestion becomes so great that suburban (not rural or small-town) development is promoted.

(iii) *Policy Implications*

The potency and apparent ubiquity of this rationalisation of service provision in rural areas may seem such that no public policy is either desirable or feasible. Perhaps market forces are inexorably, if slowly, removing the anachronisms of our central place systems. Undoubtedly, this is in large part true, but there remains a strong case for positive public policy. This case lies in the external diseconomies or social costs of the rationalisation process. First the increased affluence and mobility of the majority of rural residents means that the minority are left to some extent "high and dry" when the local pub and village shops close down. In the East Anglian *Small Towns Study*, it was argued that "to do nothing implies acceptance of decreasing opportunities in a wide sense—in terms of employment and in terms of the services and facilities which a community demands" (East Anglia Consultative Committee, 1972, p. 17). A second point relates to the costs of under-used capital in declining settlements and of continuing to provide an acceptable level of services (e.g. schooling) to uneconomically small communities—costs which are felt by the public sector and which provide a further justification for policies of intervention in the relevant market forces. Third, the uncertainty that arises from allowing market forces to decide the chronology of service rationalisation itself imposes a cost in the business of planning public investment in the affected areas.

Regarding the feasibility of intervention, a number of courses of action are theoretically open. One approach is to aim for a slowing down of the process of concentration in one of two ways. Either the present level of demand, and its likely downward trend, is accepted and a policy of subsidy is adopted with regard to service provision, or else attempts are made to stimulate the economic base and thus the support population in problem areas, in order to keep up with rising thresholds. Clearly, each of these alternatives, even if feasible, would be extremely costly in terms of the subsidies and subventions that would be necessary to persuade the private sector to choose locations which are not profitable.

The alternative approach, of course, is to accept the strength and the economic desirability of the continuing concentration of personal services and to attempt to mould change in ways which would reduce the social costs involved. There seem to be three possible ways of doing this. First, attempts could be made to increase the mobility of those people not benefiting from car ownership—housewives, children, the elderly, the poor and the infirm. This would presumably require a determined and open-ended commitment to subsidise public-transport networks which are at present inadequate in frequency and geographical coverage. Alternative strategies involving dual use of public vehicles (e.g. mail vans) or the promotion of car-sharing schemes have been investigated (Dept. of the Environment, 1971) and been found to have only limited potential in most areas. Second, the mobility of service provision itself could be increased ; already travelling shops and libraries are commonplace in rural counties. Mail-order shopping is increasing in popularity (National Economic Development Office, 1971) and the success of the British Open University, with 47,000 students currently working towards university degrees by correspondence and by only occasional tutorial contact, perhaps illustrates a trend which could be further encouraged. The third option is to encourage a major relocation of a scattered population into larger centres, where personal services could be viably established. This may appear the most radical alternative, but it would, of course, reinforce migratory processes already at work. Green (1971) claims, for example, that the annual level of local migration in rural Norfolk is such that within perhaps 20 years a quite far-reaching readjustment of the settlement pattern could quite painlessly be achieved.

It is this last-mentioned alternative which is usually termed a "growth-centre policy", but in all probability such a policy could only be justly pursued if attention were paid to some of the other possibilities simultaneously. In other words, the inevitability of a residual population remaining in small remote settlements, for whatever economic or social reasons, probably requires a degree of subsidy towards the costs of scattered provision, of personal mobility and of mobility of services also. But some degree of population concentration appears essential in most circumstances, a goal by no means unobtainable given the natural trends in that direction and the array of policy levers in public hands—not just control over the location of public services and the form of the transport network, but also, in Britain at least, control over the location of new residential development.

The deliberate restructuring of settlements hierarchies in this way has, in British county planning at least, usually been based on an assessment of viable population thresholds (Green, 1971). Thus planners in Norfolk decided that 5000 was the minimum size of population which would support a reasonable range of local facilities—a three-doctor practice, a home nurse and health visitor, etc. The problem is that different county planning departments define critical thresholds at quite different sizes: "key village" policies have worked on figures from 500 to 8000 (Green, 1971). And the analysis of service provision in southern Ontario, carried out by Yeates and Lloyd (1969), indicates that although the number of business types present in a village or town increases less than proportionately with increases in the support population, there do not appear to be any obvious "critical" thresholds at which several services become viable at once and beyond which there is little or no improvement in provision until another threshold is reached.

It seems, then, that rather too much attention can be diverted to a careful examination of population thresholds. An absence of an obvious clustering of thresholds at specific sizes has produced a wide range of estimates of critical sizes of settlement towards which policy should be directed. And, of course, examination of present thresholds reveals a situation which may be neither desirable nor feasible as thresholds continue to rise. In any case, marked regional variations in the distribution and density of population, in the terrain and pattern of accessibility and in the institutional arrangements which govern the organisation of education and medical provision, etc., appear to rule out any general solution.

Nevertheless, it might be useful to mention briefly three attempts that are currently being made to regroup a scattered population in order to be better able to maintain a reasonable level of service provision. In northern Sweden a regrouping policy has been promoted since 1965 in order to check migration to the south (Bylund, 1972). In addition to a few large growth centres on the Baltic coast, a number of what Bylund terms "sustenance places" are being established inland, each the focus of a support population of at least 3000 people. Bylund claims that research has indicated this to be a significant threshold in service provision, but notes that about forty new jobs will need to be established annually in each centre if the support population is to continue to rise in accordance with rising thresholds.

The Newfoundland Resettlement Programme (Courtney, 1972) is similarly based on the problems of service provision in the context of a rapidly declining demand for labour in the primary sector—in this case, fishing, and to a lesser degree forestry and mineral extraction. A feature of this policy is the financial incentives which are available to people who move to selected reception centres, which vary considerably in size, many having fewer than 1000 inhabitants. Between 1965 and 1971 about 18,000 people were resettled at a cost of over $8 million.

In East Anglia, policies of deliberate discrimination between villages, if not between small towns, are now well established. The Norfolk Interim Settlement Policy (Norfolk County Council, 1972) is based on a four-fold categorisation of the development prospects of all settlements, on the grounds of their present size and service endowment and their location. The study of the problems of certain small towns and rural areas in East Anglia (East Anglia Consultative Committee, 1972) highlighted the "gradual process of decline of an economic and social system" (p. 2) and recommended a package of policies to be pursued by central and local government, designed to stimulate growth in selected "growth points". Significantly, perhaps, the authors of this study did not make clear whether the centres they stressed as particularly suitable to assistance, Fakenham and Diss, were to be developed at the expense of other similar towns, or were simply representative of a larger, and as yet unspecified, selection of small growth points in the region.

CONCLUSION

It is clear that in the discussion of growth centres as selected centres for the efficient provision of services and the regrouping of a scattered population, the scale of the places involved is generally much smaller than that of growth centres in the context of efficient investment in infra-structure and even more so than growth centres conceived as means of fostering the diffusion of innovations. Policies of spatial concentration appear to be required at quite different scales and on quite different grounds, at various levels of the hierarchy. Indeed, it is the importance of the notion of hierarchy that comes out most clearly from this review of growth-centre policies and the provision of services. Ideas of optimum urban sizes in the context of public policy, whether in relation to service provision or public investment, seem to have little validity. Much more attention needs to be paid to the various objectives that a region's urban system is intended to attain, and to the costs and benefits involved in expanding particular centres within that system, in the context of those objectives.

CHAPTER 5

Agglomeration Economies and the Stimulation of Growth

THE review of growth-centre policies in Scotland, Ireland and France (Chap. 2) revealed clearly that in the forefront of the various justifications advanced for such policies is the notion that spatial agglomeration is a potent factor in stimulating economic growth. Growth centres were promoted in order that the growth of the region or nation would be greater or faster or more assured (or all three) than that which would have occurred had the initial investment been more geographically scattered. A number of reasons are usually advanced to account for this belief, but essentially they relate to the alleged advantages of large urban scale for *innovation* (discussed in Chap. 3), *import substitution* (with firms buying a greater proportion of their inputs locally), *indigenous industrial expansion* and the *attraction of industrial firms* from other regions or nations. The present chapter examines first the theoretical basis of claims that urban growth is likely to be self-reinforcing in these ways. Then it reviews the available empirical evidence relating to the role of urban size in this context and to the possible existence of crucial sizes beyond which such benefits accrue in disproportionate measure.

AGGLOMERATION ECONOMIES

In the theory of *growth poles* (briefly discussed in Chap. 1) great weight is placed on the ability of the "pole", usually a large innovating firm, to stimulate, by means of the "external economies" which it generates, the growth of a large number of other firms to which it is linked. Such external economies occur when the average unit costs of the linked firm are reduced, because of the growth of the growth-pole firm. Thus forward-linked firms are able to buy their inputs more cheaply if, having innovated, the growth-pole firm reaps economies of scale and chooses to lower its prices. Backward-linked firms enjoy scale economies themselves, because of their increased sales to the growth pole. "Laterally induced industries", whose output depends on the income generated by the pole and by its forward- and backward-linked industries, also benefit. So, too, does the "capital goods sector" which, because its level of output varies essentially with the growth rate of other sectors, is stimulated by the accelerator effect. So a large number of firms benefit from the external economies generated by the operation of a growth pole (Thomas, 1972).

However, it is important to reaffirm the point made in Chapter 1: growth-pole theory is not directly concerned with geographic space. The discussion of the effects of external economies given in the preceding paragraph is included in order to underline for geographers and planners concerned with the geographical dimension that the beneficial effects of external economies do not by any means always require firms to be geographically clustered. Sometimes they do, and these particular external economies may then be considered to be "agglomeration economies". Thus, "in the specific case of agglomeration economies, the external economies experienced by a production unit derive from its particular *locational* association with a larger scale spatial cluster of economic activities" (Lloyd and Dicken, 1972, p. 130). In addition, agglomeration economies also include certain economies which are *not* external in the above sense, namely *internal* economies of scale (those accruing from a firm's expansion, on site, of its *own* output) and *transfer economies* which arise from reductions in transport and communication costs because of physical proximity to customers and suppliers. Figure 5.1 sets out this interpretation of the meaning of "external" and "agglomeration" economies.

If internal economies of scale are considered outside the concern of the growth-centre theorist, given his interest in the *interaction* of firms and groups of firms, then three types of agglomeration economy remain relevant. First, there are *localisation economies*, which are economies of scale external to the firm but internal to the industry; second are *urbanisation economies*, which are external to both firm and industry; and third are *transfer economies*. Each will be discussed below, though with an

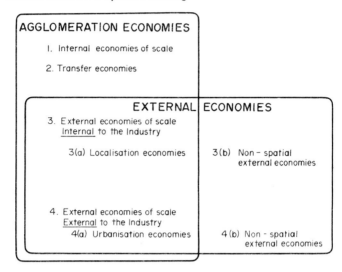

FIG. 5.1. The author's interpretation of "agglomeration" and "external" economies.

enormous literature on this subject (see reviews by Townroe, 1970; Smith, 1971; Lloyd and Dicken, 1972) our concern will be simply to demonstrate the main elements of the process by which spatial agglomeration occurs and to provide an introduction to an appraisal of empirical work which relates the scale, speed and certainty of growth to the agglomeration economies that urban centres afford.

(i) *Localisation economies*, being external economies which are internal to an industry, arise from and to some extent stimulate the clustering of similar establishments. Of particular importance are those special requirements which no single firm is able to sustain, but to which each firm contributes. A pool of skilled labour, with particular defined skills, provides the best example. Specialist subcontract services, such as electroplating and toolmaking, provide another example. Indeed, growing specialisation and the practice of putting out to subcontract those activities which yield low or risky returns is a force for further concentration if the client appreciates the problems that can arise from inadequate coordination. On the other hand, in those industries in which plant size is tending to increase, such economies are likely to be internalised: the importance of localisation economies apparently varies inversely with the prevailing size of plant.

(ii) *Urbanisation economies*. Examples of urbanisation economies are those arising from easy access to technical education facilities, to business services such as advertising agencies, and to a large and varied labour force. Regarding labour availability, for instance, similar percentage levels of unemployment would conceal the larger and probably more diversified labour pools in the bigger towns. And such towns would probably have the technical education facilities and the range of urban amenities to enlarge the labour pool, by retraining and inmigration respectively. The general point is that urbanisation economies accrue from the growth of the town as a whole—not just of the firm's like-minded neighbours.

So important are the advantages to many firms of easy access to a range of services provided by the public and private sectors that in recent years there has been a shift among urban growth theorists away from the "export base" notion that the driving-force of urban growth is the performance of its "export" sector towards a fuller appreciation of the role of the town's service sector in sustaining and augmenting the level of economic activity. Thompson has argued that the true economic base of a large city is "the creativity of its universities and research parks; the sophistication of its engineering firms and financial institutions, the persuasiveness of its public relations and advertising agencies, the flexibility of its transport networks and utility systems, and all the other dimensions of infrastructure that facilitate the quick and orderly transfer from old dying bases to new growing ones" (Thompson, 1968, p. 53). In addition, the provision of cultural and recreational amenities is demand-oriented and therefore correlates closely with the number of people sufficiently close to make use of them. If such amenities are poor, the ability of firms to attract and retain the necessary personnel is limited and many foresighted firms might in consequence be deterred from moving to or expanding in small town locations because of this. So such amenities must themselves be considered to contribute to urbanisation economies.

Examination of the way in which locational decisions are made in the real world adds further support to the hypothesis that great importance is attached to urbanisation economies and to the other benefits of large urban size. "Evidence is mounting that such factors as access to metropolitan living, social amenities, environmental preferences and economies of urban agglomeration are important determinants of location, probably more important than rates of return to capital, transport cost advantages, cheap labour costs and other key elements in traditional location theory" (Richardson, 1973b, p. 5). It is well known that the assumptions in classical location theory of perfect knowledge and of the primacy of the profit maximisation objective are rarely met in industrial location decision-making. Imperfections of knowledge enhance the attractions of well-known locations. Uncertainty about future risks and a desire to ensure at least a satisfactory (not the largest possible) profit lead to "play-safe" decisions. Personal location preferences, the desire to maximise "psychic income", draw industrialists to areas rich in the amenities that they favour. All three factors effectively amount to discrimination in favour of established urban centres.

It was this range of attractions, urbanisation economies in the widest sense, that led Hoover to conclude "I can think of several good reasons why both private and public locational preferences and decisions these days may be giving more attention to size of place (level in the urban hierarchy) and less attention to choice of region" (Hoover, 1969, p. 356). He continued, "if true, this would imply that economic activities may be expected to be increasingly footloose between major regions . . . and less footloose in regard to size of community; and consequently, that public policy may operate with increased lee-way (but perhaps diminished urgency) in inter-regional terms, and with increased constraint (but perhaps increased urgency) in terms of the choice between different sizes of urban centre" (p. 356). This is an extremely important suggestion and one to which this present chapter is largely devoted.

Of course, no one disputes that in general terms the availability of urbanisation economies correlates with size of town. The really interesting questions are whether such economies increase disproportionately with urban size (Fig. 5.2a) and whether thresholds occur, with the onset of fresh economies "bunching" together at critical sizes (Fig. 5.2b). And do net diseconomies eventually set in ? Some theorists believe that the attractiveness of urban centres for industrial location, when plotted against city size, gives a U-shaped curve, with the initial advantages of urban scale discussed above being eventually outweighed by the onset of costs deriving from traffic congestion and inflated factor prices (land and labour particu-

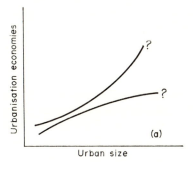

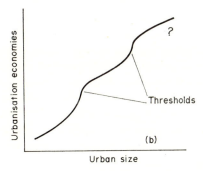

FIG. 5.2. The increase of urbanisation economies with urban size.

larly) (Evans, A. W., 1972). But all the indications are that for the individual entrepreneur concerned only with the private costs and benefits of urban size, net diseconomies arise only in the very largest towns, if at all (Alonso, 1970). Of course, this will depend, among other things, on the nature of his business and on the geographical extent of the "town" being considered: a Birmingham engineering firm moving 15 miles to Redditch New Town may still be part of the conurbation as far as his access to urbanisation economies is concerned.

(iii) *Transfer economies.* Some writers (e.g. Bergsman *et al.*, 1972) consider the economies derived from locating close to markets and suppliers to be one sort of "urbanisation external economy" in that they derive from the advantages of the locality, not from the performance of other firms in their own industry. A "purer" definition of external economies, one which reserves the term for economies deriving from the *growth* of other firms or groups of firms, runs counter to this, but probably in our context this is an arid point: transfer economies are a potent force in spatial agglomeration and hence require our attention.

We should include within "transfer economies" all those savings which derive from proximity between firms buying or selling to one another, economies which relate to the cost both of transporting goods and materials and of communicating information. The relevant costs include not only those directly involved in transportation and transmission, but also potential losses in production or in sales due to delays, and the more intangible costs which arise from ignorance of new developments in markets, materials, etc. Probably these latter factors are becoming more potent agencies of agglomeration than the narrowly defined transport costs revered in traditional location theory: "in modern industries, except in a few cases, transportation is of little practical importance, (but) communication in the narrower sense of the word tends to be more and more important, (hence) . . . the tendency for cities to grow even faster than they have grown already" (Klaassen, 1970, p. 115). Klaassen continues: "urbanisation is, in fact, nothing more than a rational process for the creation of activity bundles that can operate efficiently as bundles at a small distance from each other".

(iv) *Social and cultural transformation.* There is one further way in which territorial agglomeration affords conditions favourable for faster or greater economic growth, and that lies in the propensity of large urban centres to inculcate values and attitudes conducive to such growth. This subject is closely tied to the question of "why the social climate of cities is particularly conducive to the generation and adoption of innovations, economic as well as social, cultural and institutional" (Hermansen, 1972a, p. 186), a subject taken up in Chapter 3, but some further remarks are necessary.

It is nearly 20 years since Lampard (1955, p. 82) asked "Have cities in some way generated a dynamic force making for socio-economic change?"—a question which may seem trite today, but which at the time ran counter to the conventional wisdom that towns were largely a passive index of economic growth. Hoover "replies": "Cities serve an important role in the development process simply by being places in which people from other parts of the same region or country are brought together in densities and living conditions sharply contrasting with those of the rural areas. Conservative traditions and outlooks that persist in the hinterland tend to dissolve rather quickly in the urban melting pot: the results are always conducive to more rapid social and economic change, though they are often painful . . ." (Hoover, 1971, p. 149). One of the ways in which a city promotes this change derives from its facility for originating, relaying and absorbing new ideas, an ability which stems largely from its social heterogeneity and its talent for communication. And, according to Friedmann (1969, p. 16), the city has also "not only invented the concept of unlimited opportunity, but also . . . internalised it as the basis for its own unique culture". Of course, much of the literature on the role of cities in social transformation relates to the developing world where the transition required is indisputedly greater. But can one not at least hypothesise the relevance of this notion to growth-centre policies, say, in the Scottish Highlands or the Durham coalfields, where a tradition of life in scattered and rather inward-looking communities is likely to have bred a set of attitudes and aptitudes at variance with those demanded by modern industry?

CUMULATIVE CAUSATION, RATCHETS AND SPURTS

So far, we have looked at individual aspects of agglomeration and at the advantages it confers. Now it is necessary to introduce two new ideas, first that these individual forces interact and reinforce one another, second that in the process of urban growth the rate and certainty of growth may themselves be in part dependent on the amount of growth already achieved.

The cumulative and self-reinforcing nature of urban growth has been so much documented in the literature that only a summary account will be given, based upon a diagram (Fig. 5.3), which is itself a hybrid of those produced by Pred (1966), Keeble (1967) and Goodall (1972). The diagram indicates that the establishment of a new exporting firm is likely to have three direct effects: an increase in the employment and hence population of the town, the stimulation and perhaps the attraction of firms whose goods and services it requires, and an increase in the tax base of the community. Each of these effects leads to an expansion in the town's economic

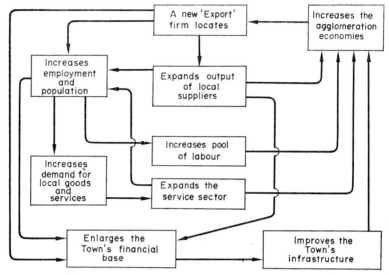

FIG. 5.3. The cumulative process of urban growth (after Pred (1966), Keeble (1967) and Goodall (1972)).

activities, whether in the manufacturing, service or construction sectors, as shown in the diagram. And each expansion increases the total demand for services of various kinds—and the money available to provide them. All the time "deposits" are being made in the town's "bank" of agglomeration economies (note the number of arrows entering the "agglomeration economies" box) which new exporting firms periodically decide to exploit.

However, while the broad outline of this model of urban growth appears valid, there is a good deal of uncertainty about the extent to which such a process is likely to continue. Clearly, it is a matter of considerable relevance to growth-centre policies to know whether at some critical stage the process tends to slow down, stop and even perhaps go in reverse, because of the onset of net external diseconomies. Only careful empirical analysis of the fortunes of large cities can resolve this issue.

An alternative view is that "perhaps some critical size exists, short of which growth is not inevitable, and even the very existence of a place is not assured, but beyond which absolute contraction is highly unlikely, even though the growth rate may slacken, at times even to zero" (Thompson, 1965, p. 22). This is Thompson's famous "size–ratchet" hypothesis, with past growth being "locked in" by urban expansion. Thompson gives five reasons why this should be so. First, size generally brings diversification and the insurance against decline that goes with it. Second, it provides a market which new firms might be attracted to exploit, and subsequently expand to serve "export" markets as well. Third, it increases the pool of leadership and entrepreneurship, and hence the possibility of innovation and the development of new industries (see Chap. 3). Fourth, it ensures a strong political base, and the ability to press for government support. Fifth, it makes more likely a favourable government response to such pressure, because of the size of the stock of capital which the city's infrastructure comprises. Other reasons might, of course, be added to these—for example, the pool of urbanisation economies discussed at length above. In addition, and this is a factor receiving increasing attention among location theorists, there is the mental image that large centres produce in the minds of entrepreneurs. Lloyd and Dicken (1972), after considering the locational decision-making processes of industrialists, conclude that many try to emulate the experience of their more adventurous predecessors, with success breeding further success in certain locations. More important, they suggest that before it reaches a certain size, a town may fail totally to figure in the industrialist's "mental map", and thus not even be a "starter" in the industrial attraction stakes. They stress (p. 178) that "agglomeration is as much a behavioural as a strictly economic phenomenon, heavily dependent upon the nature of information flows in space and the imperfections of the decision making process".

Of course, the difficulty for the theorist is to assess the *relative* importance of sheer urban size in providing all these attractions for further growth. "Although the faster growth of larger centres is a generally observable trend, it is not one which surrenders easily to statistical analysis . . .: a correlation analysis on centre size and growth . . . gives rather disappointing results . . . because the relationship rests heavily on *ceteris paribus*" (EFTA, 1968, p. 81). A supplementary factor in explaining urban growth rates, which the EFTA study stressed, was proximity to other centres—which again raises the question of the geographical extent over which agglomeration economies may be expected to extend. Another factor is the industrial composition of the town: industrial diversification generally correlates only very loosely with urban size. So, too, of course, does the proportion of a town's industry which is likely to stimulate further local production by means of the demands that it generates.

So much for the theories of urban growth and agglomeration, and for the various suggestions that have been made about the mechanism of growth and about the role or urban size in stimulating or assuring such growth. This discussion has deliberately been in summary form, because of the frequency with which this particular subject has been aired. Rather less attention, however, has been devoted elsewhere to empirical work aimed at testing some of the hypotheses set out above, and to this work we now turn. First we look at the evidence for industrial linkage being an active agglomerative force, then at the relevance of urban size in the attraction of new industrial and commercial activities, and finally at the more general attempts to relate population growth to urban size.

INDUSTRIAL LINKAGE AS AN AGGLOMERATIVE FORCE

A number of attempts have been made to assess how important a factor in spatial agglomeration is direct industrial linkage. Richter (1969) and Streit (1969), using data for American SMSA's and for German and French sub-regions respectively, each sought a correlation between industrial linkage, as evidenced by input–output coefficients, and spatial association. Each found a certain degree of correlation and Streit went on to seek potential industrial complexes based on those pairs of industries which were both strongly linked and spatially associated. But neither can be said to have isolated inter-industrial linkage as an *active* agglomerating force, since the observed spatial associations could have been partially due to "third-party" causes (e.g. access to a common labour pool) or else the product of factors once important, but now anachronistic. A more recent paper by Lever (1972a), however, using British data in a similar fashion, stressed that certain newer, expanding industries are just as likely as older declining ones, to be located in distinct geographical clusters. Lever identified two groups of expanding industries as of particular interest—a science-based cluster of industries (plastics, pharmaceuticals, etc.) in the Greater London metropolitan region which, however, owed its origin not to functional linkage but to the urbanisation economies that the metropolis affords, and a metalworking and engineering complex in the West Midlands. The latter group of industries does owe its existence to inter-industrial linkage, a fact borne out by "micro" studies which have highlighted the reluctance of many West Midland industrialists in these sectors to move far from their suppliers and markets (Smith, 1970).

However, more relevant in the growth-centre context would be some indication of how important industrial linkage might be in generating new agglomerations, either by drawing linked firms to a nascent growth centre, or by stimulating local purchasing by newly moved firms. Here the literature is less supportive. On the first point, all the evidence points to the conclusion that in industrial movement in Britain at least, industrial linkage is much more important as a deterrent to long-distance movement than a stimulus to relocation in areas where new markets or sources of materials might be available. Overall it has been other factors, notably labour availability and government policies, that have fashioned the recent geography of industrial movement (Keeble, 1971).

The second question relates to the likelihood that newly moved firms stimulate local suppliers. Some recent work undertaken partly by the author (Moseley and Townroe, 1973) is relevant here. This paper examined a sample of nearly 200 firms which have recently moved to new locations in East Anglia and northern England, and sought the degree to which any observed tendency to shift their purchasing to local suppliers correlated with a number of parameters relating to the firms and to their new environment. The authors found that only about 20% had, in fact, switched significantly to local suppliers in the 4–14 years that had typically elapsed since the move, but that metalworking and engineering firms and firms that had undertaken major reappraisals of their product or organisation since moving were much more likely to have switched. The evidence clearly indicated that a shift to local suppliers was the exception rather than the rule and that the nature of the firm was a more important factor in explaining such a shift than was either the size of the company, the size of the plant or the nature of the location to which it had moved. A German study of the ability of newly relocated firms to attract or stimulate local suppliers describes a similar situation: 80% of materials were purchased from suppliers more than 30 kilometres distant (Brosse, 1971). Brosse argued that German regional policies should continue to work for industrial dispersal, but should be less optimistic about the prospects of generating new industrial agglomerations.

Some further light is thrown on the efficacy of industrial linkage as an active agglomerative force by the studies that have accompanied certain attempts to foster deliberately inter-related and spatially contiguous industrial complexes. Here a central aim has been to establish a group of establishments which is sufficiently large that most of the necessary ancillary units are assured enough business to warrant their operation in that location. Clearly, this requires detailed analysis of how operating costs vary with location and with the scale of undertaking, as well as of inter-industry relationships—all this for a variety of possible contending complexes. But considerable optimism has been expressed by some authors regarding the potential of this approach. "There seems little doubt now that the most effective strategy for planned industrial development is to create a growth point (or a system of growth points), based on a carefully selected group of inter-related activities . . ." (Smith, 1971, p. 505). And yet, as far as the agglomerative force of industrial linkage is concerned, several caveats must be made.

First, the very need for comprehensive public planning with an emphasis on the simultaneous promotion of inter-related units suggests that industrial linkage, left to itself, is likely to be a weak agglomerative force. Second, the selection in many plans (e.g. Bari–Tarento (Newcombe, 1969), Central Lancashire (Livesey, 1972), New Brunswick (Luttrell, 1972)) of metalworking and engineering as the base for the complex appears to confirm the conclusion of Moseley and Townroe (1973) and Lever (1972a) that this particular industry is somewhat exceptional in its present-day agglomerative tendencies. Third, and most important, increasing attention is apparently being paid to *other* agglomerative forces in justifying and formulating an industrial complex, besides inter-industrial linkage. Thus, the strategy for a complex in New Brunswick (Luttrell, 1972) was based on a study not just of direct inter-firm transactions, but also of possible *joint* demand for the products and services of other establishments and the joint use of common resources and facilities, such as public infrastructure and the labour pool. Luttrell was seeking a group of industries which would most benefit from and contribute to a wide range of advantages associated with a large urban–industrial complex. Thus, it seems that emphasis has been shifted somewhat away from direct industrial linkage towards external economies of the localisation and urbanisation varieties.

URBAN SIZE AND INDUSTRIAL GROWTH

A way of looking more comprehensively at the role of agglomeration economies in industrial growth is to examine the relationship between urban size and the attraction or expansion of industrial establishments. In effect, this comes close to examining the Hoover hypothesis mentioned above (p. 94) that urban size, rather than spatial location, is now a prime locational determinant.

Urban size, is of course, only a crude surrogate for the scale of a town's agglomeration economies (see Richardson (1973b) for a critique). We have already mentioned a number of extra factors which are relevant in this respect—industrial composition, proximity to other centres, etc. And all the indications are that agglomeration economies increase more than proportionately with urban size. Stanbach and Knight (1970), for example, showed that the *proportion* of total employment engaged in business services correlates with city size, indicating that the absolute availability of such services increases much faster than does the number of inhabitants. Such reservations are, however, details. The notion that urban size is of direct relevance to the possibility of generating further growth is central to the whole growth-centre concept. Relevant empirical evidence is examined in this section and the next, which deal with the relationship of urban size to industrial and to population growth respectively.

The present focus of attention is a town's propensity to attract the all-important "city forming" or exporting sectors. Such a focus does not contradict the Thompson hypothesis (discussed above, p. 93) that it is the "non-basic" or "city-serving" sectors which are crucial to urban growth. Quite the contrary: we are now seeking to establish how successful is a good endowment of such sectors in attracting those firms which are needed to secure its "export" earnings. Also, of course, these "city-forming" or "export" firms are by no means exclusively manufacturing—but generally attempts to influence the movement of economic activity (and to study it) have concentrated on the manufacturing sector and so this will form the focus of this section.

One attempt to relate rate of growth of employment in manufacturing to urban size (labour market areas) was made by Stanbach and Knight (1970, pp. 110–11). They found that industrial growth was most rapid in the *medium*-sized ($\frac{1}{4}$–1.6 mill.) cities west of the Great Plains, and in the *smaller* cities ($<\frac{1}{4}$ mill.) in the mid-west, south and east of the United

States. The authors made no suggestion to account for this, but perhaps it indicates the advantage of large urban size in the early stages of industrial growth and the propensity of external economies to be more geographically extensive in older established, more densely populated regions.

Other work has considered explicitly the determinants of the geographical movement of industry. Some authors have successfully applied the gravity model to inter-regional movement in Britain. Thus Keeble (1971) and Sant (1974) separately found both distance and labour availability to be highly significant factors in explaining the scale of industrial movement from the London and West Midland conurbations to destinations in the peripheral areas. Perhaps the very applicability of gravity models in this context suggests that the planners of peripheral regions can only effectively overcome the disadvantages of their eccentric location by fostering growth centres of considerable "mass"? Support for this contention comes from O'Neill (1971) who examined the distribution of manufacturing industry in Ireland between 1926 and 1966 and found: first, a clear tendency for industry to become more spatially concentrated with the passage of time, with a smaller proportion to be found in the smaller towns; second, a significantly higher survival rate of firms in Dublin and Cork than elsewhere; third, a positive correlation between urban size and the ability of a town to attract new firms.

Both Keeble and Sant, however, were forced by the nature of their data to examine industrial movement between subregions often 50 miles or more in diameter, within which a scatter of small centres could produce just as much "mass" as one large centre. (This again raises the question of the areal extent over which agglomeration economies extend, an important issue taken up below.) Some work on smaller, labour-market areas has, however, been undertaken for south-east England. Keeble and Hauser (1972) sought to explain the pattern of manufacturing growth which occurred between 1960 and 1967 within a region extending roughly 50–70 miles around (but excluding) Greater London. With 112 areal units, this study came much nearer to being an inter-urban comparison and the results are extremely pertinent. Keeble and Hauser found that (p. 28) "spatial variations in manufacturing change in the study region in recent years, whether measured by employment or floorspace indices, have been chiefly influenced by variations in aggregate and specific labour availability and in existing levels of industrial activity and specialisation". Thus, the rate of industrial growth correlated directly and significantly with the size of the labour pool and with the size and diversity of the pre-existing industrial base. The prime factor, labour availability, "involved both workers made available by population growth around London, and those unemployed in more peripheral locations . . . in addition, the availability of female workers and of workers with relatively scarce skills seems to have played important subsidiary roles".

The great significance of labour availability in channelling post-war industrial movement in Britain is reaffirmed by surveys of individual firms. In a review of those surveys relating to inter-regional movement, Keeble (1971) concluded that labour availability and government policy were of roughly equal importance in the choice of destination. At the *intra*-regional scale he found five factors of prime importance. First and foremost is proximity to the conurbation of origin, there being a very clear tendency for overspill firms to move as short a distance as possible. Secondary factors were compass direction (radial movement being the norm), local labour supply, planning controls and influences, and residential desirability. Now, four of these five factors are directly related to the external economies that urban size affords—proximity and direction indicating the tie to those of the old location, labour supply and residential desirability relating to the attributes of the new location (though, of course, the amenities concomitant with large urban size comprise only part of the ingredients of "residential desirability"—a point reiterated in our consideration of the determinants of residential migration (Chap. 7)).

Finally, a wide-ranging study of industrial movement in south-east England, one which directly contributed to a strategy incorporating large growth areas, must be mentioned (Economic Consultants, 1971). From a survey of over 1000 manufacturing establishments in the region, the consultants found that factors such as accessibility to suppliers, subcontractors and markets tended to be insignificant as locational factors. What was important, once again, was labour availability—particularly the availability of certain scarce skills. This was of great importance in the selection of a location; it prompted either very short moves, so that past employees might be able to commute to the new establishment, or else moves to larger subregional centres, where recruitment was likely to be relatively easy. It was also important in the future growth of the firm: those in smaller centres (less than 50,000 inhabitants) were much more ready to complain that labour deficiencies held back the growth of their firm.

Some work by the present author (Moseley, 1973c) on the problems experienced by firms which have moved to small and quite remote expanded towns is relevant here. Ninety-three industrialists in Haverhill and Thetford (two town expansion schemes each with about 13,000 inhabitants, 50 and 80 miles respectively north of London) were asked whether the further growth of their town was likely to be in the interests of their company. Only 5% expected net disbenefits and of the 68 (73%) who expected net benefits, the reasons given are interesting:

Reasons for Favouring Further Expansion

Expansion would:

1. Enlarge the pool of labour	57%
2. Improve the town's amenities	36%
3. Attract new business for the firm	22%
4. Lead to an improved service by suppliers	6%
5. Lead to an improvement in communications	3%

(The replies sum to over 100%; some respondents gave more than one reason.)

It is clear from the above that the prospect of new business and the related questions of access to markets and sources of materials and services were of relatively much less overall importance than those of labour availability. Both directly, by enlarging and broadening the pool of labour, and indirectly, by making possible the provision of amenities which could attract and retain labour from London and elsewhere, further growth of the two towns was much to be desired. Interestingly, a parallel survey of Thetford's *residents* (Moseley, 1973c) confirmed that the limited scope for employment (for men and school-leavers particularly) and the absence of such higher-order amenities as a hospital, adequate public transport and recreational facilities were the most keenly felt grievances in the town.

Unfortunately, rather less is known of the factors influencing the movement and operation of firms in the *tertiary sector*. However, it is clear in the British context that the pattern of movement from Central London (by far the greatest source of mobile offices) is determined mainly by the rate at which costs decline with distance from the place of origin. Operating costs such as rents, rates, wages and salaries decline rapidly at first, but hardly at all beyond 50–100 miles from London. Hence very few firms in the private sector have moved their offices from London to the Development Areas, where communication and probably non-pecuniary psychic costs are much greater (Rhodes and Kan, 1971; Hall, 1972). The problems for planners in such areas is how best to simulate the locational advantages of a site in the south-east, at the same time avoiding the disadvantages—high wages, rents, costs of congestion, etc.—which prompted the move. Daniels (1969) suggested that more inter-regional movement might be forthcoming if "office centres" were identified, as part of a regional strategy, where attention could be focused on, for instance, the housing, labour training and communication requirements of office development. Unfortunately, the largest provincial cities, such as Leeds and Cardiff, which are most suitable in terms of communications and the availability of specialist services, frequently have higher salary costs than do small towns close to London.

The public sector, however, is better able to steer any offices able to move out of central London, beyond the attractive small towns in the metropolitan region, to the assisted areas in Wales, Scotland and the North. With regard to the locations within such areas which might prove attractive in this respect, the recent "Hardman report" on the dispersal of government work from London (Hardman, 1973) is instructive. Hardman proposed that 31,000 civil servants could be moved from London if an element of loss in efficiency were set against such benefits as easier staff recruitment and the creation of job opportunities in less prosperous regions. In the selection of locations the main criteria, besides the objective of favouring the assisted areas, related to efficiency: there should be good communications with London, adequate office accommodation and good prospects of recruiting labour locally and of attracting established staff from London. In addition, attention should be paid to the desirability of moving departments to towns already undertaking related government work.

All of these criteria pointed to the selection of just a few, large towns. "To scatter staff over a large number of towns . . . would be inefficient in terms of the operation of Departments, bad for the staff concerned in prospects and career management, and of limited use to regional policy" (Hardman, 1973, p. 8). The recommended pattern of dispersal is given in Fig. 5.4. It will be seen that virtually all of the reception areas outside the south-east

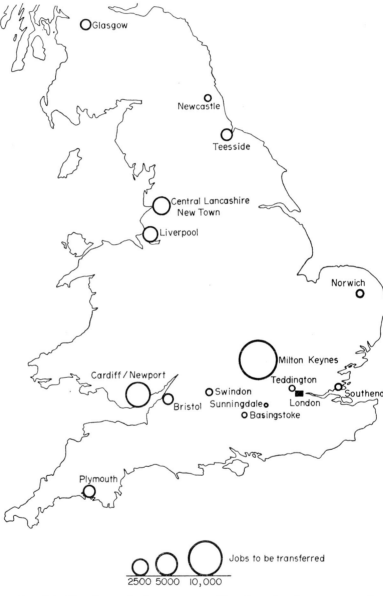

FIG. 5.4. The dispersal of government offices from London as proposed by the Hardman Report, 1973 (source: Hardman, 1973).

are urban centres with a population of at least 200,000. The only exceptions are Norwich which with its suburbs has 180,000 inhabitants, and Swindon and Central Lancashire New Town which are planned to reach 200,000 by the 1980s. This together with the information that Glasgow, Cardiff, Plymouth, Teesside and Swindon are presently vying for a slice of the 11,000 jobs "promised" by Hardman for Milton Keynes, underlines the relative strength of the largest regional centres in attracting any mobile tertiary employment.

URBAN SIZE AND POPULATION GROWTH

If we take a town's rate of population growth to be a very crude index of its ability to generate economic growth, then there seems to be value in examining the former's relationship with urban size. Does growth tend to be greater in certain sizebands? Does it tend to be more assured beyond a critical size?

Two recent studies of the growth rates of American urban systems (not just the built-up areas of towns) offer some evidence. Alonso and Medrich (1972) examined the performance of SMSAs between 1960 and 1966, and Berry (1973) that of "daily urban systems" between 1960 and 1970. (His "daily urban systems" are more numerous and geographically extensive than the officially defined SMSAs.) Table 5.1 sets out their results.

TABLE 5.1. THE GROWTH OF AMERICAN URBAN SYSTEMS IN THE 1960s

SMSAs, 1960–6 (Alonso and Medrich, 1972)		Daily urban systems, 1960–70 (Berry, 1973)	
Size band	Mean % population change	Median % population change	Size band
< 100,000	+7.6		
100,000–200,000	+9.4	−0.9	100,000–225,000
200,000–500,000	+11.9	+ 3.5	225,000–500,000
500,000–1 mill.	+11.5	+10.1	500,000–1 mill.
1 mill.–2 mill.	+14.3	+13.6	1 mill.–2,250,000
>2 mill.	+8.7	+13.7	2,250,000–5 mill.
		+12.7	5 mill.–10 mill.

Despite differences in the size bands, the time periods and the areal units that are adopted, the figures are (with one notable exception) broadly comparable. They indicate that the average rate of growth tends to increase with size up to a population of around 1 million and then level off at approximately the national growth rate (in Berry's case this figure was 13.3%).

The data also suggest, and this is more tenuous, that at somewhere in the 200,000–500,000 range growth becomes more *assured*, if not actually greater. Berry's low figures (-0.9% and $+3.5\%$) in his lowest size bands reflect the fact that he took *median* (not mean) growth rates. In other words, most urban systems in his 100,000–225,000 range actually lost population. This is masked in Alonso's and Medrich's data, where a few very high growth rates presumably pushed up the mean figures, as they readily admitted—"smaller metropolitan sizes are unstable, tending either to grow very fast into larger sizes or to lose ground" (Alonso and Medrich, 1972, p. 238). The close correlation between urban size and the *stability* of growth rates was presented graphically in some earlier work by Berry (1970a) (Fig. 5.5). And a study of the growth rates of West German cities (Klaassen, 1972) also suggested that beyond a size of about 275,000 growth rates tended to show less variance.

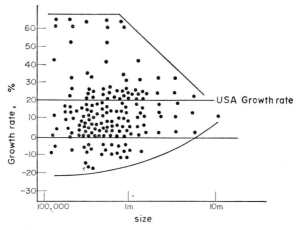

Fig. 5.5. Growth rates of American daily urban systems 1950–60 (from Berry (1970a) in *Transactions, Institute of British Geographers*, **51**, p. 40, with permission).

Does all this evidence mean that the quarter-of-a-million mark is roughly the point at which *self-sustaining* growth sets in ? Certainly, something of a magical aura has developed around this figure in the American literature. For example, Berry has stated that "the legislation establishing the Economic Development Administration set 250,000 as a maximum size for the central cities of development districts, which is entirely reasonable since above that size the necessary conditions for self-sustaining growth seem satisfied" (Berry, 1970b, p. 9). He goes on to argue that public assistance should be aimed at getting cities presently near to this size to a state of self-sustaining growth.

Shackleford has attempted a more rigorous analysis of what happens to the growth rates of SMSAs as they approach a size of 250,000 inhabitants (Shackleford, 1970, reported also in Hansen, 1972c). He considered the 100 SMSAs which reached that size at some time between 1900 and 1965, and analysed their decennial population changes with the intention of finding whether and when they underwent a population "spurt", defined as an increase of over 50,000 inhabitants in any 10-year period. He found that 88 of the 100 places experienced a spurt which straddled the 200,000 level and which on average constituted an increase of 70,000 inhabitants. It would seem somewhat suspect to consider this to reveal a crucial size at which massive growth might reasonably be expected, as it is of course highly likely that the biggest *absolute* increases in size are likely to occur near the top of the range considered—and Shackleford admits that consideration of *percentage* increases yielded no significant results. But Shackleford did observe that towns which "spurted" past 200,000 were much less likely to decline subsequently than those that passed that figure at a gentler pace: only twelve towns in the former category, all of them dependent upon a single industry, did not continue to grow.

And so, in general, it does seem that "from them that have shall not be taken away", even if it is not always sure that "to them that have shall be given" in abundance!

CONCLUSION

Three chief conclusions may be drawn from the work reviewed in this chapter—they relate to the nature of agglomeration economies, to their areal extent and to the relevance of urban size.

It seems clear that the most important single element of the agglomeration economies which derive from urban scale relates to labour availability. This is particularly true if, as seems likely, benefits of proximity to markets, suppliers and specialist services normally extend over a much greater distance than the typical journey-to-work hinterland from which most labour must be drawn. Both Cameron and Reid (1966) and McCrone (1969) suggest that for many technical external economies much of Central Scotland (80 miles across) might be considered as a single growth centre. And the present author (Moseley, 1973b) has observed the advantages that firms in individual small towns in East Anglia derive from the growth of industry in other expanding towns located within a radius of about 30 miles. Subcontractors are often found quite easily within this area and national suppliers are attracted to the area as a whole, either by establishing a central outlet at a strategic location or by making frequent deliveries which would be uneconomic if the market were one small town alone. So the possibility arises that a *group* of quite widely spaced towns might prove effective in the attraction of further industry—unless labour availability is crucial.

Some of the important questions surrounding the areal extent of the benefits of agglomeration economies may be summarised with the aid of a diagram (Fig. 5.6) in which operating costs are shown to increase with distance from the source of agglomeration economies:

(i) How great is "a", the reduction in costs, attributable to a location in town X?

(ii) How far is "b", the distance to which some degree of cost-reduction extends?

(iii) What determines the angle "c", which indicates how rapidly the external economies are dissipated?

(iv) What is the shape of the curve "d"—is it linear, concave or convex? Is it stepped?

Obviously, it would be too much to expect empirical analysis to give clear answers to these questions: the answers will vary with so many factors relating to the region and to the firms concerned. But the graph provides a conceptual framework which might be applied to each constituent of the mass of benefits which comprise agglomeration economies.

Finally, despite the doubts that this concept of gradual transition casts

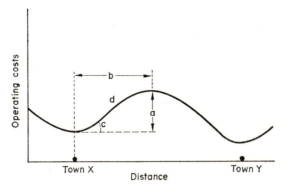

Fig. 5.6. The spatial extent of agglomeration economies.

upon the relevance of the mass of a single isolated town, the other main conclusion must relate to urban scale. A great deal of uncertainty surrounds the idea that a crucial threshold exists, beyond which self-sustaining growth is virtually assured, and that a population of around 250,000 marks such a threshold. But it does seem proven that a clear correlation exists between size and the *probability* of *some* further growth, even if the magnitude and rate of growth are less easily explained. Concentration of effort in urban areas with at least, say, 200,000 inhabitants seems to offer a greater likelihood of success, if the prime objective is moderate but continued expansion in the region as a whole, than do alternative policies of greater dispersal. But two final points must be made. First, there seems no valid reason why such an urban concentration might not take the form of a number of settlements close enough to form a single labour market. Second, the importance of urban size in providing the external economies that industries need may vary considerably from industry to industry. Some industries such as textiles (Evans, A. W., 1972) tend to prefer small-town locations and so the promotion of a *range* of urban sizes within a region may be consistent with a desire to provide the best possible urban environment for industrial growth (Morrill, 1973b).

CHAPTER 6

Growth Centres: Their Spatial Impact

SOME attention has already been paid to the spatial impact of growth centres when in an earlier chapter we considered the degree to which growth impulses are transmitted from town to town through a national urban hierarchy. In the present chapter, however, we examine in much greater detail the contention that the benefits of growth-centre expansion spread beyond the latter's immediate confines. We look at the various processes by means of which such impact might take effect and at the available empirical evidence relating to the extent, speed and form of those processes.

This is an important subject for three reasons. First, as was indicated in our introductory appraisal of the growth-centre concept (Chap. 1), many theoreticians incorporate the notion of spatial impact into their definitions of the term. Thus Boudeville (1966, p. 11) defined a regional growth pole as a "set of expanding industries located in an urban area and inducing further development of economic activity throughout its zone of influence" and Nichols (1969, p. 193) used the definition, "an urban centre of economic activity which can achieve self-sustaining growth to the point that growth is diffused outward into the pole region and eventually beyond into the less developed region of the nation". Second, the assumption that growth centres *do* benefit much wider areas appears implicit in public policies designed to stimulate extensive development by concentrating upon a few favoured places. Indeed, the political acceptability of such discriminatory policies may in part rest upon the notion of spatial impact. By way of example, it may be relevant to note in this context that in the terms of reference for a study of the desirability of building a large new town in Central Lancashire, the Minister of Housing and Local Government wrote: "in addition to providing for long term overspill needs . . . (the new town) . . . should contribute to the industrial revival of the whole region" (Matthew and Johnson-Marshall, 1968, p. 1) and the consultants duly concluded that the new town would be "a generator of economic growth and rising prosperity . . . spreading outwards to the region as a whole". This favourable assessment of the new town's impact upon such stagnant towns as Burnley and Accrington, 20 miles distant, has been strongly refuted by Batty (1969) (see p. 137 below), but the point here is that such an assessment may seem vital if discriminatory policies are to be readily accepted by peripherally located communities. The third justification for a careful examination of the impact notion concerns our general level of ignorance on this subject: "the idea is that economic improvement initiated in the growth centres will spread to their less urbanised hinterlands . . . but actually we do not yet know much, particularly in quantitative terms, of the way in which a favourable economic effect is propagated from an urban growth centre to the surrounding territory, or the range and speed of the various impacts" (Hoover, 1969, p. 352).

TWO RELEVANT MODELS

Our examination of the evidence regarding growth-centre impact derives its structure from a prior consideration of the centre–periphery model of economic development and of the theory of the spatial diffusion of innovations. The *centre–periphery model* is a general term relating to work by Myrdal (1957), Hirschman (1958), Friedmann (1966, 1969) and others regarding the processes by which spatial disparities are narrowed or accentuated. Robinson and Salih (1971) argue that the role of growth centres in regional development is simply a special case of the more general model: "in essence the growth-pole model depicts the transmission of economic prosperity as the result of two sets of opposing forces. On the one hand, growth tends to concentrate in some centre and erodes the economy of surrounding areas; on the other hand, development spreads over surrounding areas as the result of growth in the centre"—all this in the "area in which the centre and surroundings interact, the growth space" (Robinson and Salih, 1971, p. 303). Thus the vital question concerns the relative strength of these two sets of opposing forces, the forces of increasing concentration being terms "backwash" or "polarisation" and those of dispersal "spread" or "trickle-down". A great deal has, of course, been written on the centre–periphery model, but at least a brief exposition of its main tenets seems necessary, as it provides the best conceptual framework for what follows.

"Backwash" relates specifically to the tendency for the factors of production to be drawn from periphery to centre, setting up vicious and virtuous circles respectively. The more enterprising elements of the peripheral community are attracted by the supposed superior opportunities for labour or entrepreneurship in the centre ("supposed" because the superior returns may in fact be more apparent than real (Hirschman, 1958, pp. 184–5), but this point need not detain us). Similarly, capital and raw materials are drawn to the centre to fuel the latter's expanding economy. These forces have already received attention in our consideration of the nature of agglomeration economies (Chap. 5).

In contrast, "spread" relates to the tendency for initial disparities in the surface of economic development to be evened out. The relevant processes may be predominantly economic, social or political in nature. A useful categorisation of the major economic processes has been given by Yeates and Lloyd (1969) in their estimation of the total employment effects of a programme of industrialisation in part of southern Ontario. Their model, based on earlier work by Hansen and Tiebout (1963), separates the total effect into three parts, "direct, indirect and induced". Thus

$$M_i = E_i + \sum_{j=1}^{n} E_{ij} + \sum_{k=1}^{m} E_{ik},$$

where M_i = total employment generated by industry i,

$\quad E_i$ = employment "directly" created in industry i,

$\quad E_{ij}$ = employment "indirectly" created by the demands of sector i on sector j,

$\quad E_{ik}$ = "induced" employment, created by the final demand impact of industry i on the final demand sector k.

In this form, of course, the model is non-geographical, but if we consider that all the direct employment is located in the growth centre, then it stimulates three questions which are central to our concern with spatial impact. They are: Where have the "direct" workers come from? Where is the "indirect" employment located? Where is the "induced" employment located? To elaborate, all directly created workers not originally living in the growth centre itself must have been drawn to their new place of work either as commuters or as migrants. Although in one sense alternative means of journey-to-work, there is a potential crucial difference between commuting and migration, in that in the latter case workers are severed from daily contact with their original residence. Two possible consequences might flow from this severance; either their outmigration has the favourable effect of reducing unemployment or under-employment and so raising *per capita* incomes in the area of origin, or it robs that area of a source of income and of vitality with deleterious implications for its eventual development. The relative applicability of these alternatives in a given case is a matter of the greatest importance to regional planning. Regarding the location of indirectly created employment, our prime concern is to establish the degree of proximity of such employment to the growth centre and the determinants of such proximity: or, conversely, how much of the multiplier leaks away from the immediate region, and why. With "induced employment" the need is to trace the flows of income and, more important, of expenditure generated by the growth centre—certainly of expenditure by the "directly created" workers and, ideally for a full assessment, of expenditure by "indirect" and indeed "induced" workers also. Again, the concern is with the amount of leakage away from the region and with the spatial pattern within the region of the locations where induced employment is generated.

A further economic means by which a growth centre might stimulate further development in nearby areas relates to the decentralisation of capital, typically in the form of a branch plant establishment. This appears most likely to follow from rising factor costs in the centre or from the costs of coping with traffic congestion. So the degree to which firms establishing in a growth centre subsequently throw out branches into the periphery will also need attention.

Economic activity might also be stimulated in peripheral areas by government intervention rather than free market forces. This might take the form of private industrial expansion being diverted from the centre by a variety of "sticks" and "carrots", or else a policy of discriminatory purchasing of materials and services—for example, by means of a requirement that government agencies have to purchase a certain proportion of their materials from the periphery. Alternatively, the government might invest in public infrastructure over and above that consistent with present levels of demand, or else insist on national standards in the operation of such services as education and health, despite their more expensive provision away from the main centres of population. In each case, the periphery would be benefiting from a level of economic activity greater than that which a *laissez-faire* policy would have generated.

Finally, there is what Richardson (1969, p. 425) termed the "socio-economic function of growth points . . . to transform social attitudes through the zone of influence and to make economic growth more likely in the future . . . by the incentives of higher wages making local workers more productivity minded (and by) . . . showing local entrepreneurs the possibilities of growth and highlighting the existence of investment opportunities". Thus the establishment of growth centres in backward regions might, it is argued, have a demonstration effect, producing in time an erosion of conservative values, and thence a stimulus to economic growth. This mechanism has received considerable attention in the context of developing countries (e.g. Misra (1972) on India, and Friedmann (1966) on Venezuela).

In the gradual geographical spread of the propensity to accept change, the *theory of the spatial diffusion of innovations* may have much to offer. Indeed, Berry (1972, p. 108) has argued that "the role played by growth centres in regional development is a particular case of the general process of innovation diffusion and therefore the sadly deficient 'theory' of growth centres can be enriched by turning to the better developed general case". In the present context, of course, we are concerned neither with the "macro" diffusion of innovations within a system of urban places, nor with "micro" diffusion within a single small community, but with what Brown (1972a) terms "meso" diffusion—that applicable to the transmission of the effects of growth within the hinterland of a single urban centre. Further, we are no longer interested in what were termed in Chapter 3 "entrepreneurial" innovations, i.e. those whose adoption has immediate implications for persons other than the immediate adopter, but with "household" innovations which influence only the immediate adopter—at least in the short term. The hope is that the theory of innovation diffusion will permit a better understanding of the likelihood and timing of a peripheral resident's behavioural change in a way which may be construed as "development". If proximity to a growth centre emerges as an important determinant of such change, then the spatial impact of the latter is proven.

Of course, the examination of such impact must be based on an appreciation of what constitutes "development". One relevant innovation might, for example, be an input to an ongoing economic activity, e.g. a new fertiliser or corn hybrid or, more generally, a change from traditional to commercial agriculture. Similarly, the decision of a farmer or a rural housewife to sell their labour in the growth centre might be considered an innovation and be subject to the conceptual framework of diffusion theory. But the relevant aspect of development need not be directly productive; it may involve the purchase of a new consumer good and we shall examine below empirical work on the spatial diffusion of television sets in Sweden and America. Finally, a more real index of "development" might be provided by innovations relating to the development of human resources—to educational and health improvements widely construed. Innovation diffusion theory, with its well-developed set of constructs, seems particularly useful in conceptualising the spread of development impulses, though we shall discover below that there has been relatively little hard empirical work on the diffusion of developmental innovations in the hinterland of single urban centres.

Concluding this review of the processes by which growth centres might promote peripheral development, it may be useful to express diagrammatically the hypothesis that "spread" effects emanating from growth centres normally outweigh any "backwash" effects. The idea is that with the passage of time, levels of development become spatially more even (Fig. 6.1a) rather than more uneven (Fig. 6.1b). It will be appreciated that in these figures no index of "development" has been suggested, nor any numerical values placed on the distance axis. Examination of this hypothesis and consideration of the distance factor await our empirical survey below.

But of course, one celebrated attempt has been made in the literature to suggest the typical product of the interaction of the forces of "spread" and "backwash". Friedmann (1966) has presented a typology which

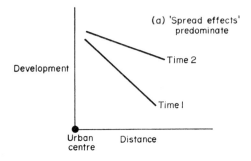

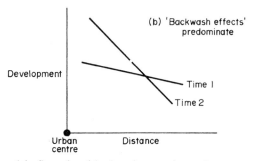

FIG. 6.1. Spread and backwash around an urban centre.

describes a sequence of regions with common prospects and problems emanating from the various centre–periphery processes, a sequence, moreover, which he claims to be widely applicable and independent of scale. Up to five inter-related regions may be discerned:

(a) *Core regions* or "metropolitan economies with a high potential for economic growth" (p. xv). Friedmann refers to a hierarchy of core regions, each the driving force of the region in which it is set. Our "growth centre" appears analogous.

(b) *Upward transitional areas*, whose "natural endowments and location relative to core regions suggest the possibility of greatly intensified use of resources" (p. xvi). They are typified by increasing investment, net immigration and increasing capitalisation of agriculture.

(c) *Downward transitional areas* are "areas of old-established settlement whose essential rural economy is stagnant or in decline and whose peculiar combination of resources suggests as optimal a less intensive development than in the past" (p. xv). Their distinctive features include net and selective out-migration, an ageing and unfavourable industrial structure, low agricultural productivity and a generally low standard of living.

(d) *Resource frontier* and (e) *special problem* regions are self-explanatory, possible additions to the essential centre–periphery model propounded by Friedmann.

Thus, from the above theoretical review there emerges the general hypothesis that around any given growth centre a broadly concentric series of regions might be expected, the major feature being an "upward transition zone" close to the centre where spread effects predominate, with a "downward transitional zone" beyond. Such zones would be arranged in broadly concentric form, except where interrupted by localised resources or barriers, channels of communication, other urban settlements, etc. This model is very generalised, however, and raises a number of more specific questions which are of great importance for a fuller appreciation of growth-centre impact and which provide a focus for our consideration of relevant research:

(i) What is the *relative importance* of the various "channels of impact" set out above?

(ii) *How much* impact is normal within the urban region surrounding the growth centre? (Conversely, how much "leakage" is there out to other regions?)

(iii) *How far*, geographically, does the growth centre's effective hinterland extend? And is it in fact true that "the spatial incidence of economic growth is a function of distance from the central city . . . (and) . . . troughs of backwardness lie in the most inaccessible areas" (Berry, 1969, p. 288)? More specifically, with reference to impact via the labour market, is it true that spread effects are confined essentially to the commuting hinterland, with a relative deterioration of living standards beyond, in the areas of net out-migration?

(iv) *How quickly* are spread effects effectively experienced within the growth centre's hinterland?

(v) *How "low"* are spread effects channelled within the hierarchy of settlements in the hinterland ? Is it true that within a given urban region growth impulses continue to be transmitted down the urban hierarchy to the smallest centres, or is such transmission essentially areal in form, or else "upward", back to the growth centre and to external larger centres ?

Obviously, these five basic questions, relating respectively to the nature, scale, extent, speed and hierarchical level of growth-centre impact, must necessarily be considered in the light of each of the various channels of impact detailed above. But common to each of these channels is an implicit series of further questions concerned with the *determinants* of each of the five "dimensions" of impact. Clearly it is vital, if the beneficial regional impact of growth centres is to be fostered as a planning objective, to know what measures can be applied in both the centre and the periphery to bring about such impact. Clear, unequivocal answers to all these questions cannot be expected, but it still seems useful to ask them.

The framework used below for the examination of these questions derives chiefly from the "direct", "indirect" and "induced" categorisation of effects discussed above. This framework cuts across the most apparent division in the relevant literature on urban impact, a division between, on the one hand, studies of *process* which focus on the various "flows" or "channels" emanating from the centre and, on the other hand, studies of *form* which attempt to relate the "surface" of development to growth-centre proximity. The latter seek to infer causation from statistical analysis rather than trace causation by observation. Each type of study has its contribution to make.

IMPACT VIA THE LABOUR MARKET

There is, of course, a wealth of studies which have charted the impact of individual factories or small industrial towns upon the local labour market in rural areas. Such "micro" studies, based upon direct observation and the use of interview techniques, have stressed the ability of rural industrialisation to reduce under-employment and to raise *per capita* incomes within the recruitment zones of the factories. Attention has been paid to the age, sex and skills of the labour recruited, to the effect of raised incomes on consumption patterns and to the overall impact upon the traditional agricultural sector of a reduced workforce and a new source of capital. Typical examples of such studies relate to the United States (US Dept. of Agriculture, 1961), France (Bertrand, 1970), Germany (Kotter, 1962) and Ireland (Lucey and Kaldor, 1969). The present author has, for example, noted that two small towns in East Anglia, industrialised primarily for the benefit of ex-London firms and residents, now draw between one-quarter and one-third of their workforce from the surrounding areas (Moseley, 1973b).

However, these "micro" studies, being detailed but isolated case-studies, are of limited value in answering the basic questions set out above. The ability of rural industrialisation to improve the lot of displaced agricultural workers is not in doubt, but such studies say little about the possibility of impact beyond the commuting hinterland, of the relative importance of impact via the labour market and of such issues as size and spacing in growth-centre policies. "Macro" studies, relating observed indices of growth or development to other factors, appear more fruitful in this context.

Ruttan (1955) and Nicholls (1961) found that in the American South the efficiency of the local labour market was much the most significant factor in explaining spatial disparities in personal income levels—both among agricultural workers and among other rural residents. With counties in the eastern half of the USA being typically 10–15 miles in radius, the fact that rural prosperity correlated closely with the level of urban and industrial development *in the same county* strongly suggested the greater effectiveness in raising *per capita* incomes of occupational mobility and the commuting to local non-farm employment, rather than residential mobility in the form of migration from more distant areas. Despite high levels of migration from non-industrial areas, Nicholls found a widening gap in farm income levels at the county level. It appeared that only in counties offering substantial opportunities for commuting to non-farm employment was rural under-employment being reduced at a significant rate. This was due partly to the rapid redeployment of surplus labour and partly to the increasing capital investment in agriculture in such counties, made possible by the new source of income.

Moreover, Hodge (1966), examining the spatial pattern of prosperity in eastern Ontario, found a clear correlation between the indices of "non-farm poverty" which Berry (1965) had earlier derived for the rural areas of that region, and his own indices of "poor urban development" for the towns contained by those areas. In other words, there was a clear interaction between urban and rural prosperity, leading Hodge to advocate some kind of growth-centre policy to promote rural development. However, it should finally be noted that this discussion relates to urban impact on rural *prosperity*: at least one study has shown that in the short term urban expansion may surprisingly raise unemployment levels in the vicinity, with rising activity rates and immigration responding initially to the increased demand for labour (Laber, 1972).

In short, a number of studies have pointed to the much greater reluctance of agricultural workers to shift to secondary and tertiary employment if this involves migration, and to the apparent inability of outmigration alone to effect a substantial improvement in the situation of remote rural areas. A depressing scenario of the effects of migration from such areas has been outlined by Parr (1966). Migration robs the area of the youthful, ambitious and skilled elements of the community and so reduces the ability of the areas to attract new industry or to sustain the expansion of pre-existing establishments. Further, migration sets in train a downward spiral of multiplier effects, causing contraction in establishments which serve the local market. And a declining tax base necessitates either a poorer level of service provision or higher rates of local taxation, either outcome reducing further the attractiveness of the area. In all, it seems irrefutable that away from the main urban centres, relative levels of prosperity and prospects for development are cumulatively diminished, but it is important to try to give precision to the expression "away from the main urban centres". What is the extent and gradient of the urban impact, and what sort of urban centres are relevant in this context?

Taking variation in total population as a crude index of development in rural areas, there is, of course, a great deal of evidence to show that such variation is dependent at least in part upon proximity to major urban centres. For example, Rikkinen (1968), examining the growth and decline of population between 1930 and 1960 in an area within 70 miles of Duluth, found that while in the 1930s villages tended to grow throughout the study area, irrespective of location, thereafter there was a clear inverse correlation between growth and distance from Duluth, with the transition from net growth to net decline occurring at about 10 miles (1940–50) and 20 miles (1950–60) from the regional capital. The extent of the inner zone of growth he attributed to the process of suburbanisation: the crucial factor was ability to participate in the Duluth labour market while living some distance away.

Variation in total population, considered alone, is, however, only one possible index of development. Berry has shown quite conclusively that, in fact, a large number of such indices correlate quite closely with access to major urban centres or, more accurately, with the propensity to commute to such centres (Berry, 1968, 1970; Berry and Neils, 1969). Berry produced a series of maps and cross-sectional traverses (Fig. 6.2) which showed that "varying rhythmically with the degree of participation in metropolitan labour markets were a variety of other variables: population densities, value of farmland and buildings, income and education levels, migration rates, patterns of population change and degrees of unemployment" (Berry and Neils, 1969, p. 275). He showed that only where commuting fields overlapped were rural welfare levels maintained at relatively high levels. And he claimed, on the basis of this work, that only towns with more than 25,000 inhabitants had any significant effect upon these gradients.

Some more detailed work on the determinants of the spatial pattern of *per capita* income change has been undertaken by Nichols (1969) using data on percentage variation between 1950 and 1960 in the median family income of each of the counties of Georgia. Arguing that a large proportion of such variation could be "explained" simply by rising population, both variables being linked to expanding employment opportunities, Nichols focused on the spatial pattern of the *residuals* from a regression of income variation upon population variation—in other words, she was concerned to explain the pattern of particularly high increases in income levels. The map of residuals (Fig. 6.3) revealed that such increases were clustered around the major cities, especially Atlanta (population about 500,000) and, to a lesser extent, Macon, Chattanooga, Savannah and one or two other large towns. Visual inspection of this map suggests that perhaps 40 miles marks the maximum extent of these zones of particularly rapid increase in prosperity.

Not all studies seeking to explain levels of prosperity in rural American counties, however, have succeeded in establishing the influence of urban centres as much as 40 or 50 miles away. Logan (1970), examining indices of rural prosperity derived by principal components analysis for counties in the Mid-West, and Sears and Dymsza (1969), examining percentage variation in median family incomes in a wide scatter of American counties,

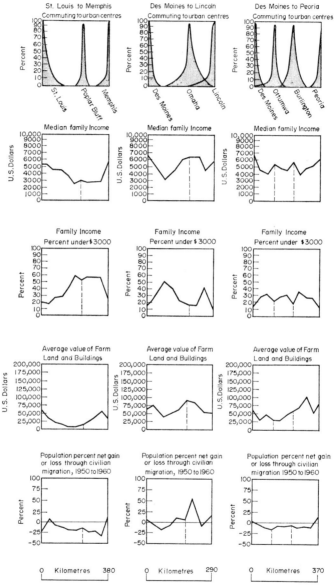

Fig. 6.2. Gradients of urban influence in the United States (from Berry (1970a) in *Transactions, Institute of British Geographers*, **51**, pp. 30–31, with permission).

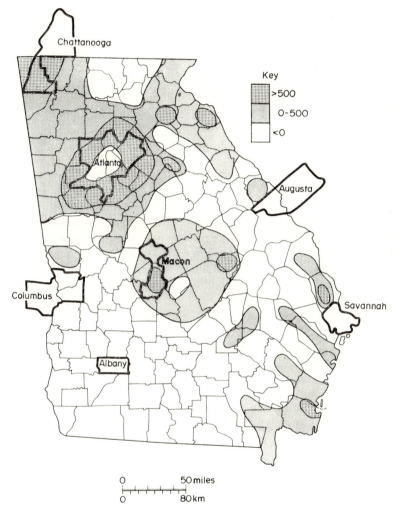

Fig. 6.3. Residuals from the regression of increases in median income against increases in population, Georgia, 1950–60 (from Nichols (1969) in *Environment and Planning*, **1**, p. 205, with permission).

each sought to relate these measures to the proximity and mass of neighbouring urban centres, and they failed. At least their correlation coefficients, though frequently in the "right" direction, were statistically insignificant. Much more significant were indices relating to the *same* counties for which observations of levels of prosperity were made—variables relating to age-structure, education levels and unemployment (Sears and Dymsza) or to the degree of local urban development (Logan)—findings much more in keeping with those of Nicholls (1961) and Ruttan (1955), discussed above. It may be that the American county is generally too coarse an areal unit for a fine-grained analysis of the gradient of urban impact.

It was with this problem in mind that the present author turned to rural France to test hypotheses relating to the spatial impact of growth centres (Moseley, 1973a). Attention was focused upon Rennes, the regional capital of Brittany, a town which has doubled in size to around 200,000 inhabitants over the past 30 years, with major expansion of its industrial and tertiary base. Brittany as a whole exhibits most of the features of a peripheral, essentially agricultural region—sustained net outmigration (at least between 1911 and 1968), income levels well below the national average and a high dependence upon declining economic sectors. The analysis was of the form of a generated surface of socio-economic development within the *département* of Ille-et-Vilaine, which extends very roughly 40 miles around Rennes in each direction and lies on the eastern edge of the Brittany region. Its main attraction from a statistical point of view is that it contains over 350 communes, for each of which a wide range of data is available.

By performing a principal component analysis upon fifteen variables which related to the level and progress of development in the *département*, an underlying "index of development" (Fig. 6.4) was extracted, which loaded significantly and positively on measures of net migration, expansion in the building sector, and the proportion of households with baths or showers, central heating, telephones, cars and domestic running water. It loaded negatively on a measure of the importance of agriculture as a source of employment. Then, trend surface analyses were performed in an attempt to disentangle systematic trends from less significant local variations. Separate analyses on each of four quadrants of the *département* were undertaken and the four "cubic" surfaces, together with traverses through them, originating at Rennes, are reproduced as Figs. 6.5 and 6.6. These

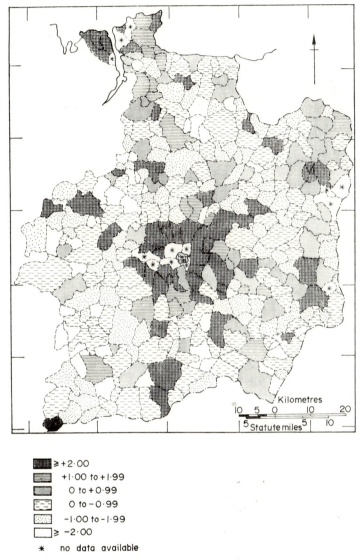

≥ +2·00
+1·00 to +1·99
0 to +0·99
0 to −0·99
−1·00 to −1·99
≥ −2·00
* no data available

Fig. 6.4. An "index of development" in Ille-et-Vilaine, France (source: Moseley, 1973a).

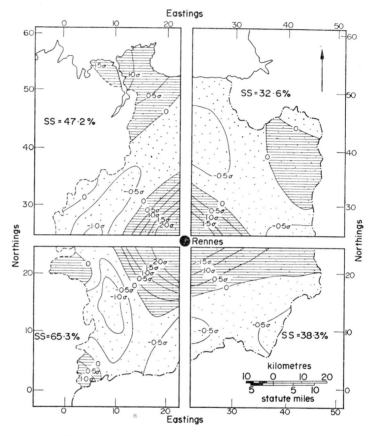

FIG. 6.5. The "cubic" trend surfaces in Ille-et-Vilaine (source: Moseley, 1973a).

"cubic" surfaces statistically explained between one-third and two-thirds of the variance in each quadrant: they describe the underlying form of the surface of development.

With a full description of the work available elsewhere (Moseley, 1973a), only the main findings will be mentioned here. The first is that proximity to Rennes was indeed the main determinant of the level of development. Second, other towns with over 25,000 inhabitants (St-Malo and Fougères) clearly "pushed up" the surface in their vicinity: towns in the 10,000–25,000

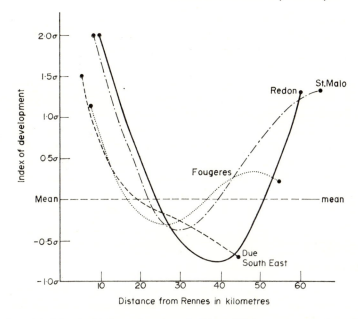

FIG. 6.6. The "cubic" trend surfaces in Ille-et-Vilaine—traverses through the four quadrants (source: Moseley, 1973a).

range may or may not have been significant in this respect, the evidence being equivocal. Third, the extent of the zone around Rennes containing high scores on the index of development was quite narrowly confined. Beyond only 12–15 miles, the picture was one of declining employment opportunities, net outmigration, a declining number of food shops and building trade establishments, of low levels of domestic amenities and car ownership, and of very little new industry. So Friedmann's "upward transitional area", that area showing the "possibility of a greatly intensified use of resources", appeared closely confined to the essential commuting hinterlands of the main towns in the *département*, although some extension of this 15-mile radius was noticeable along the main axial routes.

It does seem, then, that on the basis of all available evidence, the possibility of daily journey-to-work to "large" towns is the most important single determinant of the level of prosperity in rural areas. In addition, it is clear that the level and probably the spatial extent of growth-centre impact depends to some extent upon the size of the centre, though it is not proven that below a certain minimum size impact is disproportionately small, despite both Berry and the present author suggesting a possible discontinuity at around 25,000 inhabitants. A further point upon which doubt must remain is whether there is a critical proportion of a rural area's workforce that must commute to an urban centre for a "reasonable" level of prosperity or development to be maintained. Morrill (1973b) suggested that this proportion should be 10–20% in order to "bring an acceptable level of welfare", a figure which applies to those communes 12–15 miles from Rennes in the author's study. But the existence and precise identification of meaningful discontinuities or thresholds, both of growth-centre size and of distance from growth centres, appear less important than the basic conclusion that the ability to commute to major centres is the most relevant factor.

INDUSTRIAL LINKAGE

Although it appears clear that the extent of its commuting hinterland is the main determinant of a growth centre's impact upon the level of prosperity in surrounding rural areas, this is not to say that growth impulses might not be channelled by other means to certain locations within or beyond the commuting hinterland. In particular, we must look also at the creation of "induced employment" by the spending habits of growth-centre workers (see below) and, in this section, at the propensity of growth-centre firms to buy materials or services from within the region in which they are established. It is, indeed, backward linkage which is most important in this context: the amount of "leakage" of such purchases being a crucial factor in the stimulation of regional growth. (Lever (1972b) has, for example, noted one assessment of the problems of promoting growth in Scotland: "regional policies in Scotland may be likened to trying to fill a bath with the plug out!") Forward linkage *may* be an important stimulus, if the provision by growth-centre firms of cheaper or more accessible inputs stimulates peripherally located firms to greater levels of production. Less is known about this, but the stimulus is likely in most circumstances to be small.

The fact is that empirical studies of the spatial pattern of inter-firm linkage in Britain suggest that except in certain trades, mainly in the

engineering and metalworking sectors, *local* purchasing tends to con-
stitute only a small percentage of the total (for a discussion of this, in the
context of agglomeration economies, see the previous chapter). A number
of studies of linkage in areas where high hopes of a strong multiplier effect
were entertained bear this out. Yeates and Lloyd (1969) examined the
effect of a programme of industrialisation in the Georgia Bay area of
southern Ontario. The establishment of thirty-one new establishments,
employing over 2000 workers, had generated only about twenty extra
jobs in linked firms, in a zone extending 40 miles away. The vast majority
of materials was purchased from major industrial centres elsewhere in
North America. Admittedly, these findings referred to the situation
only 2 years after the establishment of most new plants in the area. (The
time factor is something to which we shall have to return.)

An extremely detailed study of a carefully selected sample of twenty-four
firms in West Central Scotland (Lever, 1972b) is particularly interesting
because it showed that despite that region's considerable industrial endowment, it provided in all only about 15% by value of the inputs to the
selected firms. And only 20% of purchases were made in the whole of
Scotland. Examination of the experience of major car-assembly plants
moving to the industrial areas of Merseyside (Salt, 1967) and Central
Scotland (James, 1964) confirms that within 4 or 5 years of their establishment there was still considerable reluctance, or inability, to make use of
any local suppliers of materials and components.

The previous chapter (p. 101) reported a survey of nearly 200 firms
which moved 4–14 years previously to the Northern and East Anglian
regions. This survey confirmed that with certain exceptions, mainly firms
in the metalworking and engineering sectors, it was quite normal for
relocated firms to retain their old suppliers, even if this meant "stretching"
their links over distances of 100–300 miles. And even where some shift to
local suppliers occurred, the overall multiplier effect was likely to be
small. The ninety-odd manufacturing firms which moved between 1959
and 1971 from London to Thetford and Haverhill, two overspill towns in
East Anglia, still purchase in all less than 10% by value of their purchases
in that region. Most of the multiplier effects leak to London, elsewhere
in Britain or abroad (Moseley, 1973b).

Of course, much of this empirical work relates to the situation existing
in a relatively short period of time, rarely more than 5 to 10 years after

the move. But the general equanimity with which the retention of traditional suppliers was regarded suggests that the *status quo* might well be expected to continue for some considerable time. And regarding the local spatial pattern of any intra-regional links that were established, the East Anglia evidence (Moseley, 1973b) indicates predictably that any impact was largely felt in the largest towns in the new region, or else in other expanding small towns. "Problem" small towns were hardly affected at all (Figs. 6.7 and 6.8).

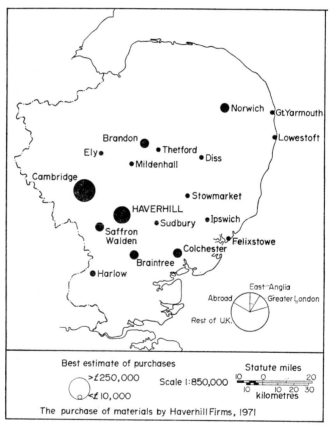

Fig. 6.7. The sources of materials purchased by Haverhill Firms, 1971 (source: Moseley, 1973b).

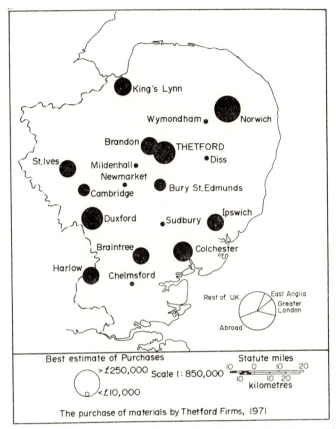

Best estimate of Purchases

> £250,000   Scale 1 : 850,000

< £10,000

Statute miles

The purchase of materials by Thetford Firms, 1971

Fig. 6.8. The sources of materials purchased by Thetford firms, 1971 (source: Moseley, 1973b).

There is rather less evidence regarding the likelihood of growth-centre firms establishing branch plants within the region in which they are located. But Smith (1970) has shown that for most Birmingham firms moving or establishing branches, even a move of 20 or 30 miles away from the external economies of the agglomeration may appear prohibitive. She found that only about 35% of all metalworking firms leaving their previous site in Birmingham moved outside the city boundaries. In the East Anglian context, the present author found that four out of nearly 100 new firms in Thetford and Haverhill had already established branch plants elsewhere in the region because of shortages of land or labour. None of these branch plants employed more than thirty workers, but this might represent the early stages of a significant "spin-off". Certainly, some longer-established firms in East Anglia with heavy labour requirements (an electronics firm in Cambridge and a number of Norwich shoe firms have thrown out branches into rural pockets of female labour. More research is needed on the determinants of the spawning of local branch plants.

PERSONAL EXPENDITURE

Rather similar questions need to be asked about purchases made by the workers whose employment derives directly or indirectly from the establishment of the growth centre. To what extent do these purchases create multiplier effects within the region, and more specifically, which parts of the region are likely to be most affected? Do such effects "trickle down" to the smallest and most distant settlements, or is some other process likely to be at work? Hoover (1969, p. 352) has, in fact, advocated a policy of steering new development *away* from the main urban centres on the grounds that "the purchases of the hinterlands from the . . . centre . . . would automatically create at the centre additional income and employment in the whole range of central place activities". Similarly, Nichols (1969) predicted that income multiplier effects would probably gravitate towards the major centres, especially as rising incomes tend to be spent on non-essential, higher order commodities. This is the hypothesis which we must examine: "trickle up" or "trickle down"?

Much more is now known about the spatial pattern of such effects, following the widespread application in British planning practice of the Garin–Lowry activity allocation model. This model takes as given a certain distribution of basic employment and seeks the distribution of residential development and service employment that is likely to ensue. To derive this, the model uses two interaction models of the gravity type in which journey-to-home and then journey-to-shop are simulated, given assumptions about the relative attractiveness of different residential areas and shopping centres and their distance away. The model is iterative, in that the estimation of subsequent "rounds" of service employment is also included in the final estimate of total impact. The details of the model need not concern us (Cordey-Hayes and Massey, 1970), only its typical output.

A very interesting application of the model was made by Batty (1969) in an attempt (referred to above, p. 115) to predict the likely impact of the proposed Central Lancashire New Town upon an area of north-east Lancashire, 10–25 miles away, which suffered from a declining economic base and net outmigration. By modelling the likely trips for journey-to-home and shopping purposes, Batty showed that it was likely that much of the service generation would occur in the new town itself and, to a lesser extent, in Blackburn, a large town only 10 miles away (Fig. 6.9). He argued that for any service employment to be generated further afield it would be necessary to shift a large portion of the new basic employment out of the new town.

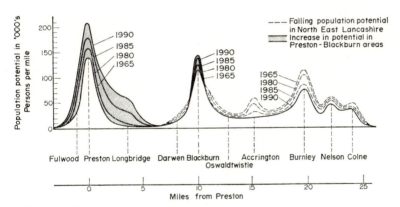

FIG. 6.9. North-east Lancashire, estimated population potential profiles, 1965–90 (source: Batty (1969) The impact of a New Town: an application of the Garin–Lowry model. *Journal of the Town Planning Inst.*, **55**, p. 434, by permission of the editor).

The present author used the conceptual framework of the Garin–Lowry model in an intensive examination of the "first round" of the impact of the growth of Thetford and Haverhill in East Anglia (Moseley, 1973b). By means of appropriate surveys it was established first where the workers in the new factories lived and second where they shopped for various commodities. A synthesis of the destinations of shopping trips made by the residents of Thetford and Haverhill and by commuters to those towns, for both "convenience" and "durable" commodities, is set out in Figs. 6.10 and 6.11. What emerged was that in each case about 75% of the workers in each town usually bought "convenience" goods in the growth centre and 50% also bought most of their "durables" there. Trips away from the growth centres were primarily to larger centres such as Norwich, Cambridge and Bury St. Edmunds, or else, to a lesser extent, to the ring of small towns 6–16 miles away where some commuters bought some convenience and durable commodities. Overall, the generation of service employment was seen to have benefited: first the growth centres them-

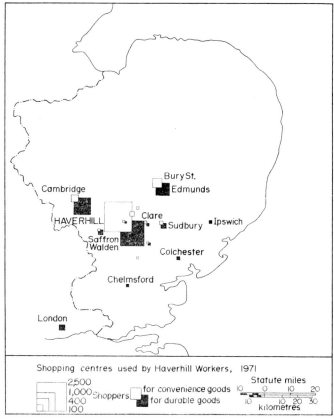

FIG. 6.10. Shopping centres used by Haverhill workers, 1971 (source: Moseley, 1973b).

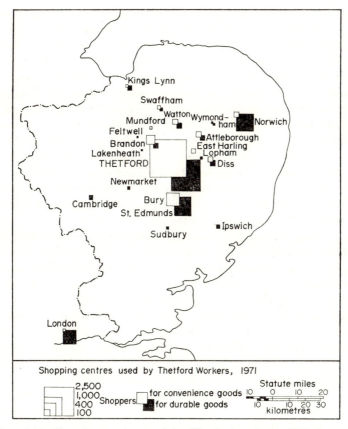

Fig. 6.11. Shopping centres used by Thetford workers, 1971 (source: Moseley, 1973b).

selves, second the large regional centres 12 to 30 miles away, third the ring of small towns, and fourth the neighbouring villages. It seemed that very few commuters spent substantial amounts in the village shops and that generally trips away from the growth centre were made only in order to benefit from the greater attraction of the larger centres. As was concluded at the time (Moseley, 1973b, p. 93), "certainly the expansion of the two small growth centres has improved the choice of employment and presumably the prosperity of many residents of the small towns and villages surrounding them, but in terms of the generation of supplementary economic activity, such impulses appear to have trickled up."

Confirmation of these findings has come from a study of eighty-six American labour market areas ("functional economic areas"), each with central cities with between 25,000 and 100,000 inhabitants (Lewis and Prescott, 1972). An attempt was made to explain the level of activity in the retail and other service sectors, first in the central city and then in the periphery. Regression equations indicated that whereas the scale of central city service activity was explicable in terms of the population and income levels of *both* central city and periphery, peripheral service activity was to be explained *only* in terms of peripheral population and income levels. In other words, peripheral services appeared to derive little from central city size. Lewis and Prescott's conclusion (pp. 68–69) was that "the strength of spatial spending patterns from the smallest rural towns to the central cities . . . suggests that policies promoting centralised urban growth alone will have severe impacts on commercial sales in peripheral communities. Though central city retail and service sales are substantially influenced by incomes earned in peripheral towns, the effects of increasing demand in the growth centre appear to be spatially self-contained."

Such conclusions should not, of course, be surprising in the context of central-place theory which asserts that the size of centre depends upon the purchasing power of smaller, hinterland settlements. But it does run counter to growth-centre conventional wisdom that the level of economic activity in a growth centre's hinterland depends on the scale of the former. The above empirical findings are also, of course, consistent with the tendency noted in a previous chapter for the demand for personal services and goods to be increasingly met at higher levels of urban hierarchy, because of greater affluence and the effect of this on tastes and on mobility. Finally, it may be noted that these results also concur with those of Hodge's attempted explanation of the viability of retail centres in the Great Plains of Canada (Hodge, 1965). He found that within about 15 miles of major centres there was an *inverse* relationship between distance and the likelihood of small-centre demise. In other words, the competition provided by large centres cast a "shadow" within which small centres struggled to survive.

However, one final caveat must be made. We have concentrated almost exclusively on that part of the income paid to a growth-centre worker which is spent on goods or services purchased in shops or similar establishments. A large proportion, however, will be spent on other commodities. Two which have received little attention are housing and recreation. By definition, a commuter who buys or renovates a house is spending money in the periphery (though the house vendor may take it straight out again). And if he goes camping or enjoys some other rural pursuit which costs money, then he is also channelling money into peripheral economic activity. If such expenditure could be shown to be greater than that which would have occurred without the establishment of the growth centre, then the periphery would appear to have made a net gain. More work is needed to find out whether such expenditure is significant enough to offset the clear tendency for most other expenditure to flow to the growth centre and other major urban centres.

INNOVATION DIFFUSION

Much empirical work on the spatial diffusion of innovations in a developmental context appears of limited relevance to our field of study. Studies of the adoption of agricultural innovations in pre-war Sweden placed great weight on the role of face-to-face communication as a determinant of the process (Hagerstrand, 1967). More recent studies of the spread of indices of modernisation in developing countries, such as cotton cooperatives in Tanzania and local administration in Sierra Leone (reported in Abler *et al.*, 1972), emphasise developing patterns of accessibility, but may be of doubtful applicability to advanced economies in the 1970s with much better developed networks of transport and communications.

Some work on the diffusion of television receivers in Sweden and America confirms these doubts. Berry (1972) did indeed find distance from a town that had previously adopted a TV station to be an important determinant of the proportion of rural households with television sets, but he noted that this was particularly true in the early days of market penetration—in the 1950s. By the 1960s the timing of the entrepreneurial adoption (urban adoption of a TV station) and distance from that station were largely irrelevant in explaining the "hold-out" zones of low penetration. By then a much more significant factor was simply household poverty: areas not adopting were mainly in the poorest parts of the rural south. And Berry's work on *colour* television, where the earliest adopters were located in often remote parts of the affluent south-west of the USA (Berry, 1970a), led him to doubt further the relevance of accessibility to urban centres as a factor determining the future adoption of household innovations.

Tornquist's study (1967) of the spread of television sets in parts of Sweden confirms that the distance factor was virtually irrelevant. He noted that information about the innovation was spread by extensive networks of social relationships and that a much more significant determinant was variation in "acceptance-proneness" or the degree of resistance to innovation demonstrated by individuals. Brown (1968) also played down the hypothesised role of information dissemination in his work on the diffusion of TV sets in Sweden, stressing the role of market factors, especially the distribution policy of the propagator of the innovation—which centres were selected for retail outlets—and the shopping habits of potential adopters.

So there appears little empirical evidence to substantiate *in the present day* Morrill's stimulating representation of the spatial diffusion of innovations from an urban centre as a wave-like process. Morrill (1968) suggested that the eventual spatial distribution of innovation acceptance is the product of a process of innovation adoption in which the zone of maximum acceptance moves progressively away from the origin as time processes, until the "wave" eventually peters out (Fig. 6.12). Thus, according to Morrill's model, innovation diffusion is characterised by the gradual movement of an active crest, as inner zones approach effective saturation. It would be a very valuable contribution to growth-centre theory if such

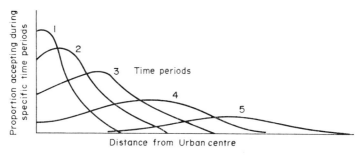

FIG. 6.12. Spatial diffusion as a wave-like process (source: Morrill (1968) Waves of spatial diffusion. *Journal of Regional Science* **8**, 1–18, by permission of the editor).

a process could be observed and charted: it is said to have applied to the adoption of automobiles in Sweden in the 1920s, but it may well not be applicable today.

Even so, in considering the possible role of growth centres in the process of development, it remains of great interest to know just what factors impinge upon decisions to adopt or not to adopt such innovations as a new production process, or a new consumer good (Brown, 1972b). Innovation diffusion theory, though it has not yet reached the stage of producing predictive models, does set out a number of the most significant relevant factors. Consider the problem from the adopter's point of view. He must be able to learn of the innovation and subsequently to acquire the innovation without undue expense. If the innovation relates to an ongoing economic activity, then he will consider any extra costs of getting the product to market—be it a new agricultural product, or perhaps his own labour if he is considering taking a growth-centre job. And the use of the innovation may require the prior establishment of suitable infrastructure—electricity if the innovation is an electrical appliance, or adequate roads if repeated contact with the town is necessary. All these factors will influence the decision and all suggest the likelihood of a distance-decay pattern of adoption around the growth centre. Indeed, if the necessary level of information reaches outlying places at progressively later dates, and if demand gradually increases at the centre for the product of the innovation, so making greater transport costs progressively more bearable, then Morrill's wave-like process might be expected.

But of course a number of factors are likely to interrupt this "ideal" pattern. There will be localised variations in the availability of information, according to the varying nature of people's movements and contacts—where they work and shop, with whom they associate, etc.—and in the degree of their resistance to change. And the physical environment might have a real effect by impeding communication locally, or by affecting the surface of production costs and therefore the potential value of introducing a new process.

So the factors which impinge upon the adoption of innovations are quite well known, but it is still not clear whether, from the potential adopter's viewpoint, it is better to be near to a number of small towns, with all the latter's disadvantages in adopting entrepreneurial innovations (Chap. 3), or to be relatively distant from an "early adopting" large town.

There is a need for much more work on the effect of different settlement patterns on the spatial diffusion of household innovations.

CONCLUSIONS

Recalling our previously defined *basic questions* about the nature, scale, extent, speed and hierarchical aspects of spatial impact, what positive conclusions have emerged? The first point is the importance of impact via the labour market. Even though the periphery may be well endowed with suitable suppliers, impact via industrial linkage is likely to be slight unless growth-centre firms have a very strong requirement for frequent contact with their suppliers. It is by the direct possibility of employment that growth-centre firms make their greatest contribution to the prosperity of peripheral residents. And we have seen that the commuting hinterland is the most important single index of the extent of the centre's impact. Suggestions have been made that certain great metropolises may systematically influence the growth rates of other towns a hundred (Semple *et al.*, 1972, on São Paulo) or even a thousand miles (Casetti *et al.*, 1971, on Los Angeles) away. But doubts have been cast on the validity of the techniques used to establish such trends (Gaile, 1973) and, in any case, cities with several million inhabitants appear qualitatively different from those normally considered as growth centres.

On the hierarchical aspect of growth-centre impact, it seems clear that there is a close relationship between size of settlement and propensity to benefit. The only towns outside the growth centre's commuting hinterland likely to receive any expenditure are those sufficiently larger than the growth centre to be able to exceed its attractions as a service centre and as a source of industrial materials. Villages and small towns within the hinterland are likely to benefit relatively little, although the occasional purchases made by commuters may be enough to effect a "holding operation": no growth in service provision may occur in the hinterland of growth centres, but possibly no decline either.

The most difficult aspect upon which to draw concrete conclusions concerns the speed of the build-up of any impact that occurs. The relevant evidence is very fragmentary. It seems clear that within 5 years of beginning operations, growth-centre firms make very limited demands upon local suppliers. But the fact that there is *some* expansion suggests that in 10 to

20 years the impact might be much more substantial, although it may be argued that if relocated firms do not feel the need to establish local links shortly after the trauma of moving then they may never need to. And the diminishing contribution of inter-regional transport to industry's total operating costs suggests that the retention of distant suppliers might, in most circumstances, be sustained indefinitely. On the chronology of recruiting peripheral workers, the evidence is equally inadequate. Examination of recruitment by firms establishing in Thetford and Haverhill indicates a 3- or 4-year initial "slack period", in which surplus labour in the towns themselves was taken up (Turner, 1966). Thereafter, an increasing number of workers was drawn from the surrounding areas at a rate which seemed to depend on the overall increase of demand for labour in the centre. Examination of such expansion is, of course, confused by the general centrifugal tendency in residential development: the numbers commuting to Thetford and Haverhill have increased enormously, but many commuters are former residents of the town or else have moved to the commuting hinterland directly from other regions. But, as a general rule, it seems that impact via the labour market is likely to be rapid as well as substantial.

What *implications for policy* can be drawn from this? Perhaps the most important point is that if commuting hinterlands mark the effective spread of significant benefits, then a *spacing* of growth centres sufficiently close that their hinterlands overlap would appear to be necessary to achieve an objective of raising the entire "spatial surface" of development. (Such an objective raises again the "place" versus "people" prosperity issue: this was raised above (p. 20) and is considered again in the concluding chapter.) Regarding the minimum *size* of centre which will have an appreciable impact on this surface, a figure of 25,000 has been suggested (Berry and Neils, 1969; Moseley, 1973a). But a good deal of doubt must surround this figure, on three counts. First it has absolutely no theoretical basis: there is no apparent reason for the scale of impact being other than directly proportional to size of centre and no apparent reason, other than two entirely inductive studies, for believing that if there is a discontinuity, it occurs at around the 25,000 mark. Second, if we accept such a breakpoint, then how do we interpret research on small expanding towns in East Anglia (Moseley, 1973b) and Brittany (Bertrand, 1970) which shows that several hundred rural residents have benefited quite clearly from the employment opportunities offered by small growth centres of 5000 to 15,000 inhabitants? Perhaps the 25,000 breakpoint marks the minimum for effecting a *discernible* impact—discernible, that is, by conventional spatial analysis of published census data. The danger of pursuing "place prosperity" is again apparent. The third point is that our conclusions on the virtual absence at the lower end of the urban hierarchy of any significant "trickle down" of growth impulses suggests strongly that a determined policy of steering growth only to towns with more than 25,000 inhabitants would ensure the stagnation of nearly all smaller towns and the decline of most smaller towns outside the growth centres' commuting hinterlands. So, depending on the specification of objectives, a strong case can be made for some latitude in the policy of concentration. Finally, a point on the *composition* of growth centres. It would seem that impact might be greatest either if the selected firms were of the sort that might tend to buy materials locally (see pp. 101 and 133 above) or if they were labour intensive and of the sort that needs large amounts of unskilled or only semi-skilled labour, since many of those requiring employment will have little industrial experience to offer.

Some further points can be made regarding measures applicable in the periphery to increase growth-centre impact. First, information: the conservatism of many businessmen regarding the sources of their supplies may reflect their ignorance of what their new region has to offer. A "buy locally" campaign might be introduced if it were found that apparently adequate local suppliers were being consistently overlooked. Second, if the prime importance attached to the labour market is justified, then policies of increasing local recruitment and of extending the commuting hinterland appear justified. This implies attention to retraining so that employers can find required skills locally, and to transport if people living more than 10–15 miles away are to be induced to commute rather than migrate. Subsidised bus transport is frequently supplied by large employers. Possibly small remote towns could themselves organise and perhaps subsidise a suitable bus service. An initial move of this sort may be necessary if a large number of people are to appreciate the advantages of taking up such employment. Alternatively, the informal sharing of cars might be promoted by organising some way by which those requiring and offering lifts might be easily introduced (Dept. of the Environment, 1971). So the general point is that interaction between centre and periphery should be facilitated by a careful policy package designed to overcome the obstacles that exist.

Considering the *research* needed to clarify many of the issues in growth-centre impact, Brown (1972b, p. 36) has said that what is needed are "sub-models for each polarisation and trickle-down mechanism, of which diffusion of innovations appears to be only one, in a growth-pole context so that eventually a theory or conceptual model of growth transmission (or not) in pole hinterlands can be constructed". With this end in mind, it may be useful to pull together a number of research priorities suggested by this present review.

Taking the diffusion of innovations first, the main priority seems to be to define just how far distance from urban centres is an important factor in determining the timing of adoption. And do waves of acceptance in fact spread out, as Morrill suggested, and, if so, at what speed? More generally, what is the relative efficiency of different combinations of the size and spacing of urban centres, if innovation diffusion is to be maximised? This last point cannot be answered until much more is known of the relative roles of urban hierarchical rank and of distance, near the bottom end of the settlement size continuum: is it important to have a well-developed central place hierarchy of small towns and villages, if spatial location is more significant in adoption?

Emphasis on the behaviour of individual "actors" might be a valuable focus for research. In particular, we need to know much more about how individuals decide to take up growth-centre employment and about what leads them to decide to commute (daily or weekly) or to migrate to their new workplace. And, considering the amount of research that has been undertaken on journey-to-work trips, there have been few attempts to predict the spatial extent of the hinterlands of individual growth centres. Theory suggests that the availability of competing employment opportunities and the facility of travel to the centre are likely to figure strongly, but these suggestions need to be formalised—especially given the thesis of this chapter, that the employment hinterland is the most important index of growth-centre impact. As well as extent, there is timing: is there a typical profile of the rate at which recruitment from a hinterland is made? Even a careful examination of published journey-to-work data (now on a quinquennial basis in Britain) could give a lead here. Finally, on commuting, we need to know more about the identity of the commuter—a rapid increase in the numbers involved might reflect migration into the commuting hinterland from other regions or from the centre, as much as an increase in employment opportunities taken up by previously under-employed rural residents.

Turning to industrial linkage, it would be useful to know more about the general reluctance of new firms to use local suppliers. How real are the fears that such firms presumably attach to the ability of local suppliers to perform satisfactorily—or is it simply ignorance that produces this conservatism? And much more needs to be known of the likelihood of growth-centre firms spawning branch plants and establishing them within the urban hinterland.

Concerning the income distributed to growth-centre workers, the pattern and implications of "non-shopping" expenditure is far from clear. And the eventual effects of taxation paid to local authorities is also an under-researched field: how far do peripheral communities benefit from facilities publicly provided there thanks to the wealth generated in the growth centre?

The final word must relate to the "place or personal prosperity" dichotomy. How true is it that small and scattered growth centres do not have a similar global impact to a few large centres experiencing equal growth in absolute terms? There needs to be resolution of the disagreement between "macro studies" which generally fail to perceive any tangible benefits from policies of scatter and "micro studies" which emphasise that 200 new jobs provided in a small town bring very real benefits—to 200 people at the very least.

CHAPTER 7

The Generation, Interception and Attraction of Migrants

ONE justification for pursuing a growth-centre policy in a depressed region relates to the supposed ability of major urban centres to generate and to attract migrants. There are three arguments here. First, it is argued that the presence of a growth centre will encourage some peripherally located people to migrate and to shift to a more productive occupation or industry, these people otherwise being content or condemned to remain either unemployed or underemployed. In other words, it is contended that on the grounds of bringing people into the labour market, a growth-centre policy is more likely to be successful than the alternatives of dispersing growth within the depressed region or of concentrating outside the region altogether in the most prosperous areas of the country. The second argument is that given the inevitability of a certain amount of migration from the most depressed parts of the problem region, and given the desirability on both social and economic grounds of diverting these migrants away from the major metropolises (premisses which we will not dispute here), then a growth-centre policy is the one most suited to undertake the necessary "interception". The third argument is that the development of our problem region is held back, at least in part, by a lack of skilled and professional manpower and that in order to attract such people from other regions the deliberate fostering of urban attractions, by means of a growth-centre policy, is necessary. These three arguments relate successively, then, to the generation, interception and attraction of migrants. And so we must look in this chapter not at the *effects* of migration on the fortunes of the growth centre and of its hinterland (subjects examined in Chapters

5 and 6 respectively), but at the *causes* and *nature* of migration. And it will be necessary to focus on migration between, not within, labour market areas.

THE GENERATION OF MIGRATION

The assumption of the first argument is that the proximity of urban centres is a major factor in stimulating the decision to move from a depressed area and that neither the scattering of small amounts of growth within that area nor the denial of any growth at all except in the country's core regions would be as successful in this. Does this assumption accord with the evidence on migration? Put differently, is the spatial disposition of growth in fact a major factor in determining the scale of migration from depressed areas?

Lowry (1966) and others have argued that in migration the decision to go and the decision on where to go are generally quite independent. Two decisions are involved and the need for the second only arises if the first one was positive. Lowry's work on migration between American cities showed this quite clearly—"my experiments indicate that total out-migration from place *i* can probably be forecast without regard for the destination of the migrants" (p. 63). He stressed that factors of distance (from attractive destinations) are *not* of particular importance in explaining the amount of migration from backward areas.

Nor, he discovered, are the economic conditions of the area of origin. This second point, in particular, may seem hard to accept, but it has been confirmed by a number of other studies. Lansing and Mueller (1967), after an extensive survey of American migrants, concluded that "low levels of employment opportunity or low income levels do not stimulate outmigration, nor do high levels of economic activity inhibit outmigration" (p. 337). Unarguably, such conditions do correlate closely with levels of *net* migration, but they do so by affecting a region's propensity to *attract* migrants from elsewhere, not to retain its own population. (More on this below.)

What, then, does determine the scale of migration from an area? The answer appears to be the proportion of its population "at risk": "the propensity to migrate is primarily a function of one's niche in the social system" (Lowry, 1966, p. 94). This niche is, in turn, primarily a function of age and of certain other demographic factors. A study of gross migration flows within west Virginia concluded: "The outflow stream is dependent mainly upon the age structure of the resident population (whereas the inflow is principally dependent upon the economic opportunities available in the area)" (Rutman, 1970, p. 208). A wealth of studies has indicated the marked propensity to migrate of people in their late teens and twenties. At this stage in the life cycle attachment to the place of birth is relatively weak and aspirations are often high. A second factor, or group of factors, relates to levels of training, education and social class. Correlated with such factors are the possession of marketable skills and of the ambition to sell them for a better price than can be obtained locally. So, as Jansen (1968 and 1969) has suggested, the propensity to migrate is a function mainly of one's stage in the life cycle and one's perceived upward mobility potential.

Studies specifically of migrants from depressed rural areas bear this out. Taylor (1969), attempting to define what made some redundant miners from west Durham move to other parts of the country, while others preferred to stay, concluded, "compared with non-migrants, migrants are those characterised by the overall qualities of dislocation and aspiration. . . . They became migrants because they aspired to a way of life which was both materially richer and more secure and were able to realise such aspirations because of an overall dislocation in their relationships with primary and secondary groups in the village" (p. 116). Hannan's study (1969) of Irish rural youth confirmed that the main factors determining the decision to migrate were first the strength of aspirations of economic and social mobility and second, the degree of attachment to the family or local community—Taylor's "aspiration" and "dislocation" factors again.

Now, if we accept that the decision to migrate rests largely on life-cycle and career-pattern factors, how relevant is a growth-centre policy likely to be? Probably not very much. It may perhaps *reduce* the need for migration felt by an ambitious person presently living within its commuting hinterland, but it is likely to be largely ineffectual with regard to the amount of migration originating further afield. Such migration appears to depend primarily on demographic and social factors beyond its control. Further, even if the pattern of urban settlements were a potent force in bringing about migration, the *scale* of extra migration that might be generated from depressed rural areas would probably be very small. In

Britain and many other advanced economies the brunt of the run-down of the primary workforce has already been borne and, more important, prolonged outmigration has tended to have already robbed depressed regions of their most mobile elements. In short, it seems that those stalwarts in depressed areas who have resisted all other temptations to migrate are unlikely to be moved by building a growth centre on their doorstep—or by any other settlement policy.

THE ATTRACTION OF MIGRANTS

If we agree with Hollingsworth (1970), who concluded in his study of migration from Scotland that "outward migration from any particular area varies relatively little and one could almost say that there is a pool of migrants each year and localities compete for them" (p. 161), then how competitive are growth centres? This question needs to be asked in two contexts: how competitive are growth centres first in "intercepting" migrants originating broadly in the growth centre's own region, second in attracting any necessary personnel from other regions? In fact, these two questions are less distinct than they might seem. As Richardson (1973a) has suggested, the separation of migration into intra- and inter-regional components is really an artificial convention: what are needed are "spatial models", not intra- or inter-regional models. And the two questions are united by a common concern to establish whether a spatial concentration of investment within a region is likely to prove more attractive to migrants than the same amount of investment more widely scattered. In other words, are *large* urban centres intrinsically more attractive?

Taking first the growth centre's interception role, it is clear that this can only be effective if *both* urban size and urban proximity are important factors in a would-be migrant's choice of destination. If only proximity were important, then the case for intra-regional spatial concentration would not be proven: migrants from depressed parts of Brittany would be as easily (or perhaps more easily) dissuaded from going to Paris by providing opportunities in any or all of the towns in Brittany as by providing them in only the regional capital, Rennes. If only urban size were relevant, then there would be no need to concentrate investment within the region of origin: Rouen (near to Paris) would be as effective an interceptor of Breton migrants as would be Rennes, a town of similar size.

Of course, the general applicability of the gravity model in this context suggests that both size and proximity *are* important. A large number of studies have shown that the amount of migration from *i* to *j* depends to some considerable degree upon the job opportunities at *j* (compared with those of competing centres and measured usually in terms of unemployment or earned-income levels) and the distance from *i* to *j*. Migration models of the "intervening opportunity" variety (e.g. Jansen (1969) on inter-county migration in Belgium) reaffirm the potential for interception of a large growth centre placed between an area of outmigration and a large alternative destination.

The propensity of migrants to prefer nearby destinations, *ceteris paribus*, is well established. There are at least four reasons (Vanderkamp, 1971) why a "near" town is likely to attract more migrants than a "far" town of identical size and composition. First, there are the monetary costs of moving and resettling, which will vary (though not linearly) with distance of move. Second is the susceptibility of information flow to the friction of distance: ignorance and therefore uncertainty are likely to increase with distance. Third are the "psychic costs" arising from the severance of kinship and friendship ties—a severance more likely and more effective with increasing distance. Fourth, there is the degree of contrast between the cultural environments of the origin and destination and this "social distance" is likely to correlate very roughly, but none the less significantly, with geographical distance.

At first sight, however, the evidence provided by gravity models on the role of urban *size* seems less convincing. While no one disputes that the labour-market conditions in alternative destinations are crucial determinants of migration flows, these conditions are frequently expressed in relative rather than absolute form. Often it is the *level* of unemployment at *j*, or the disparity between the levels at *i* and at *j*, or the change in the level at *j*, which emerges as significant—not the *absolute* number of jobs available. Thus Lowry concluded (1966, p. 94) that "for outmigrants the pattern of choice among alternative destinations is influenced by both distance and labour market conditions at these destinations. The outmigrant prefers nearby destinations and prefers destinations with low unemployment rates and high wage rates." Now it must, of course, be admitted that Lowry was concerned only with migration to SMSAs with over 250,000 inhabitants, thus taking a certain "mass" as "given", but this emphasis on *rates* and *levels* does seem to indicate that the case for having one growth centre of 100,000 inhabitants rather than four equally prosperous centres of 25,000 is not proven—especially as the overall proximity of the latter to the main areas of outmigration might well be greater.

Similarly, scholars who have stressed the "friends and relatives effect" in determining migration flows, noting that the information and assistance furnished by early migrants to their friends back home generates in time well-worn migration paths often confounding gravity model regularities, have also not proven that large centres are necessarily more attractive. Traditionally, it has been the largest centres which have had the greatest endowment of previous migrants and hence the greatest propensity for more to be attracted (Greenwood, 1969, 1970). But there is no obvious reason why the transmission of information and of promises of assistance should be less effective from our four small centres than from one big centre. The fact that high incomes, low unemployment rates and good endowments of friends and relatives have traditionally been associated with large urban centres does not necessarily confound a policy of some dispersal—so long as some way could be found of providing such attractions in smaller centres.

This, however, is probably the crux: small towns, however numerous, may in fact be unable to replicate the economic, social and cultural attributes of a single large town. Indeed, Richardson (1973a) has argued that the attractions of urban centres should form the centre-piece of models attempting to explain patterns of migration. "If it is accepted that both intra-regional labour mobility and labour inflows into a region play a role in determining its rate of growth, it becomes important to be able to offer satisfactory explanations of these movements. The argument here is merely that such explanations need to take account of the scale and absorptive capacity of urban labour markets, agglomeration economies as an attractive force to migrants . . ., distance and mobility costs, relative housing conditions at origin and destination, the leisure and cultural facilities of urban areas and other factors that can only be allowed for in an urban migration model" (Richardson, 1973a, p. 136). And he goes on to specify (though without as yet substantiating) a regional growth model in which the growth rate of labour within a region is considered to be mainly a function of the region's agglomeration economies, its wage levels compared with the national average and of the average locational preferences of its inhabitants.

In this model, specifically urban factors would be involved in two ways, first in the agglomeration economies, indicated by measures of the size and proximity of urban centres in the region, and second as one element relevant to locational preferences.

If we interpret "agglomeration economies" in this context as relating to all the economic advantages accruing to migrants from the large size of their urban destination, then it is clear that such economies may be considerable. Large towns normally enhance job choice in a number of ways—for example, by providing a selection of similar jobs so that redundancy need not mean unemployment and by offering scope for promotion to the top jobs which normally cluster in big centres. Further, it seems that large centres tend to have higher *per capita* incomes, not just because of their more favourable industrial or occupational mix, but because of the opportunities for greater productivity that external economies afford.

In addition, although "work reasons" are the predominant factor influencing the choice of destination by long-distance migrants (Harris and Clausen, 1966), non-economic considerations are important and perhaps are becoming increasingly so. A recent analysis of inter-regional migration in America (Schwind, 1971) confirmed the role of "environmental quality" in this respect, with the climatic attractions of Florida and California being particularly significant. If enough people place enough weight on such considerations, then employment location decision-makers will be forced to pay attention. The point, however, is how important an element in the overall concern for environmental quality are intrinsically *urban* attractions?

Of course, there is a good deal of evidence to suggest that the level of social and cultural amenities which only large towns are able to offer is, indeed, an attractive force. The present author (Moseley, 1973c) found a high level of dissatisfaction with the urban amenities of small expanding towns in East Anglia, both among residents who had moved out from London and among employers who were often thwarted in their attempts to attract skilled workers and middle management by the absence of cinemas, a hospital, a swimming pool and similar amenities. And there is evidence from other studies that larger urban centres may be disproportionately attractive, whether for employment or other reasons. Somermeijer (1961) found that an "index of attractiveness" was important in explaining migration between Dutch provinces, and one element of his index was the degree to which provinces were urbanised. More recently, von Boventer (1969) attempted, using multiple-regression analysis, to explain the scale of migration into German cities between 1956 and 1966. A number of factors emerged as significant which were not necessarily associated with size of town, in particular the availability of housing, the presence of expanding industrial sectors and the overall accessibility of the town, whether measured in terms of its rail connections or of its calculated "population potential". But urban size did emerge as independently significant, in three ways. First it was found that cities with over 250,000 inhabitants tended to attract migrants in greater measure than the presence of the above factors would suggest. Second, small towns near to major cities apparently benefited from the latter's external economies and attracted rather more migrants than would otherwise be expected. And, related to this point, von Boventer also observed that most remotely located small towns, particularly those with fewer than 75,000 inhabitants, were much less successful in attracting migrants.

And so it does seem clear that other things being equal, a large urban centre is likely to be more successful (per head of population) in attracting migrants than its smaller rivals. The above evidence, however, comes from studies of very generalised migration flows. It remains to consider the relevance of growth centres in the attraction of that particular group of people whose particular endowment of expertise and initiative is required in order to offset the debilitating effect of prolonged selective outmigration and to put in train a programme of development. Of especial relevance is the behaviour of those ambitious members of the middle class who are termed "spiralists" because of their willingness to move around geographically in order to move up socio-economically (Mann, 1973). Such people, who differ from the more locally orientated middle class (the "burgesses") by their lack of class ties with the local community, tend to move frequently and over long distances in order to further their careers and social status (Jansen, 1968, 1969).

Except in so far as such advanced career opportunities do tend to be found in larger towns, there is no obvious reason why urban size should figure significantly in the spiralist's choice of destination. A readiness to "go anywhere" suggests that small-town locations would not necessarily be a deterrent, if the job opportunities were available. Indeed, House *et al.* (1968), in a study of the northern business manager, found a growing tendency for new executives to seek small-town residential locations. This accords with some French research, cited by Hansen (1968), which indicated that of those Parisians who would prefer to live in the provinces, the vast majority would favour a small town or rural location rather than a home in a regional capital. It may be that environmental considerations will prove increasingly important in the choice of residence by executives, but many of these considerations may not relate to urban size. House's work cited above (1968) led him to conclude that for the north to prove more attractive to business executives, attention should be paid to landscaping, air pollution, housing quality and school facilities—as well as to the cultural and social amenities that normally require a concentrated support population.

CONCLUSION

Nevertheless, it does appear that the balance of advantages in this respect lies with the larger town which, if properly planned, ought to be able to offer a better "bundle" of environmental attractions than a more dispersed settlement structure. And if we add on the considerable employment attractions of larger centres, then the argument is underlined.

The implication of this for the planning of problem regions must be that attention should be paid to building up one or a very few major centres, as proposed for Appalachia by Hansen (1970). But there is a danger here. If, as we have seen, the urban structure is largely irrelevant in the *generation* of migration, with most "residial" unemployed or under-employed peripherally located people refusing to move, then the jobs made available in these few large growth centres may go largely to mobile workers from other regions (Alonso, 1970). If regional growth is the prime objective then such an outcome would not be undesirable, but to the extent that welfare and full employment objectives are held important then some degree of investment dispersal would still be required.

CHAPTER 8

Conclusion: Implications for Policy and Research

THE justifications for growth-centre policies reviewed in the previous five chapters are not the only ones that have been put forward in the literature. Occasionally it has been claimed that "people are happier" in medium-sized towns, an interesting assertion, but one upon which little convincing research has been undertaken (see A. J. Brown, 1972, pp. 164 et seq.). Other supposed justifications do not on closer examination *necessarily* require policies of deliberate spatial concentration. Thus Parr (1965) put forward as reasons for pursuing growth-centre policies the relief of congested cities, the accommodation of population growth and the attainment of regional balance. But if the attainment of these goals does in fact require deliberate spatial concentration then this derives from the reasons discussed above—agglomeration economies, public sector scale economies, etc.—not from the inherent nature of the goals themselves. Similarly, Neutze (1967) and Cameron (1970) have argued that a clear commitment to a growth-centre policy makes the overall coordination of policy easier. "Unless the government knows which centres are going to grow, it can only provide public services after the demand has appeared. If there is planned growth of a few centres, they can be provided, with confidence, in advance" (Neutze, 1967, p. 127). But it would appear to be the *commitment* to a defined spatial strategy, not the *nature* of that strategy, that affords the climate of certainty which is so valuable for executive action. There seems no reason why an equal degree of commitment to a policy of scatter would be less effective in this respect.

So we are left with the reasons reviewed in the previous chapters.

Policies of deliberate spatial discrimination derive from the goals of promoting the diffusion of innovations, reaping agglomeration economies, conserving public expenditure, efficiently providing consumer services, spreading benefits within a region and intercepting and attracting migrants. What lessons can be drawn from our review of the validity of these justifications? First, does the evidence point towards a critical size of centre towards which spatial planning in backward areas should be directed?

LESSONS FOR URBAN SIZE

Regarding the *diffusion of entrepreneurial innovations* (Chap. 3), there emerged a clear correlation between the likelihood of early adoption and the size of urban centre. But the social structure, location and growth rate of the centre were also clearly relevant, as was the nature of the innovation—those transmitted within large industrial corporations may be very little affected by urban size. As a general rule, however, large urban size offers the prospect of short-circuiting the normal processes of innovation diffusion. And somewhere in the population size-range 10,000–200,000 hierarchical diffusion tends to give way to neighbourhood diffusion, but it proved quite impossible to establish a generally applicable critical size in this context.

Related to this is the finding (Chap. 5) of a clear correlation between population size and likelihood of a town experiencing at least *some* subsequent growth. *Agglomeration economies*, widely construed, ensure that very few towns with more than 250,000 inhabitants subsequently decline, even if the rate and magnitude of growth are less easily predicted. The performance of substantially smaller towns is significantly more volatile.

Analysis of the public sector costs of providing *infrastructure* (Chap. 4) suggests that a minimum size (around 30,000) is desirable for most economies of scale to be reaped, but that thereafter *per capita* costs tend to increase. However, the rate of increase is gentle, at least to around 250,000, with other factors such as urban form and density proving more critical in cost terms. And so, remembering that such exercises fail to take account of the *benefits* which accompany urban expansion, the evidence on the costs of constructing and managing towns gives the planner a good deal of latitude. The particular circumstances of individual candidates for expansion appear more relevant.

On *consumer service provision* (also Chap. 4), the case for concentration rests largely on the rising thresholds of support population needed to sustain the various services. But again, it proved impossible to define key thresholds at which a substantial bundle of services becomes viable and towards which planning policies might aim. Marked local variations in patterns of accessibility, population density, purchasing power, etc., preclude the emergence of a generally applicable target size or sizes. The dynamic nature of the problem underlines this difficulty. But it is clear that growth centres in this context have tended to be towns in the 1000–10,000 size-range.

Considering *spread effects* from a growth centre (Chap. 6), impact via the labour market emerged as most important. In this context a population of 25,000 appeared to mark a possible discontinuity below which discernible spread effects are insignificant. But evidence that development impulses among small towns move generally *up* the urban hierarchy provided a case for actively diverting at least some new employment to even smaller towns, if an objective of promoting development throughout the hierarchy was to be pursued.

Urban size appeared to be a largely irrelevant factor in the generation of *migration* (Chap. 7). But it did appear relevant in the interception and attraction of migrants. Because the range of amenities and of employment opportunities correlates with urban size, a single big town is likely to prove more successful in attracting migrants than a group of smaller towns with an identical aggregate population. Again, what constitutes a "big" town in this respect is far from clear, though there was some fragmentary evidence of a qualitative change in the 200,000–300,000 range.

What does all this mean for spatial planning and for the selection of urban centres for preferential treatment? First, it reaffirms the value of policies of spatial concentration as a *guiding principle*: growth is spatially unbalanced, and, by the careful exploitation of this imbalance, a number of desirable goals can be achieved. Second, it indicates, however, that there is no single optimum size, or even optimal size-range, towards which policy should strive. To the extent that self-sustaining growth, the early adoption of innovations and the attraction of migrants from other regions are held important, then there is a strong case for promoting within a problem region an urban centre with at least 200,000 inhabitants. But, given the reluctance to migrate of the "problem people" for whom developmental policies are generally intended, then exclusive attention to the largest urban centres is likely to bring little benefits to those remaining in the interstices, beyond the commuting hinterlands of the largest centres. So a strong case can also be made for steering at least some new employment opportunities to smaller towns in strategically placed locations and with clear growth potential. Positive intervention is required to achieve this, as hierarchical "trickle-down" cannot be relied upon.

But is there a minimum viable size for these smaller towns? This is a difficult question, but the evidence on the economics of public investment and on spread effects within commuting hinterlands suggests that 25,000 might be a useful "rule of thumb". At least, the onus of proof should lie with advocates of specific towns below this order of magnitude. All of this discussion, however, relates to centres for basic employment provision: there will probably remain a need to restructure the pattern of consumer service provision by means of policies of discrimination between urban centres much smaller than this.

Perhaps a cluster of small towns, planned as a single growth area, would provide the best of all worlds? "It is not necessary that a growth centre be limited to one city. A system of cities or towns linked by adequate transportation and communications might serve as well, or better" (Hansen, 1972b, p. 122). The advantages of enlarging the extent of spread effects and possibly of reducing public sector expenditure (Stone, 1973) could be coupled with the agglomeration economies of large overall size. Such a solution appears attractive, but the main drawback relates to labour availability. We have seen (Chap. 5) that perhaps the major attraction of large urban size for most mobile manufacturing firms is the pool of labour available to them. And so only if the cluster of towns were sufficiently compact to act as a single labour market area would this attraction remain. Thus, such a strategy has only limited potential for overcoming the concentrate-or-spread dilemma.

Inevitably, the conclusion has to be that it is the whole urban hierarchy that has to be considered and in some sense "optimised": individual growth centres cannot provide all the answers. In most regional planning situations there will be a need for major regional centres with the greatest potential for attracting new investment, new ideas and new people from other regions; smaller centres providing employment opportunities in more peripheral areas; and local centres performing a clear service function.

Each sort of centre will have its own role to play in the process of development.

Furthermore, the issue of where in the urban hierarchy attention should be primarily directed can only be resolved given a clear exposition of the goals of the planning exercise and of the deficiencies of the particular region in question. The need for careful goal specification is central. If national goals are paramount, particularly the goal of overall economic growth, then a much greater degree of concentration will probably be required than for the more regional or local goals of full employment, a more equitable distribution of income and the minimisation of unnecessary migration. An urban strategy requires a prior resolution of the "efficiency or equity" dilemma. Thus rather than the blind pursuit of a "growth-centre" policy of steering new development to one or a very few centres, the need is to generate a number of alternative strategies, incorporating different combinations of concentration and dispersal, and different selections of specific towns for favoured treatment, these strategies then being evaluated in terms of the expressed objectives.

The urban strategy selected and the exact degree of concentration practised will depend secondly, of course, on the particular circumstances of the region in question. In particular, there are the different needs of a "never-industrialised" backward region and a "developed-but-distressed" industrial region. The former, probably with a pattern of settlement developed to serve a largely primary economy, will probably need a radical restructuring of the spatial disposition of its human and capital resources, with emphasis placed, initially at least, on building up at least one urban centre of sufficient magnitude to prove attractive to investment and migrants from other regions. The second type of region will probably already have centres sufficiently large for this purpose, but a good deal of rebuilding might be necessary if the infrastructure is obsolete and if the largest towns are, in fact, centres of net diseconomies. In this case, the evidence on urban size relating to infrastructure costs, spread effects and service provision would appear relevant in shaping the new spatial strategy around the old urban cores. Again the need would be to generate alternative strategies with varying degrees of concentration and to test them against a predetermined statement of objectives. Thus the general thrust of the argument is that the planner's task should be more the restructuring of the spatial pattern of resources in a given context of local circumstances and predetermined goals than the "implementation of a growth-centre policy". As was argued in Chapter 1, growth-centre policies must be made-to-measure, because they do not come ready-to-wear.

So far, urban strategies have been discussed in a single-region context. In fact, a strong case can be made for *national* urban strategies and for the application of the lessons of growth-centre policies to the selection of centres for preferential treatment at the national level. Pressure for nation-wide urban strategies has come from two directions. One argument (put forward by Hansen (1970) in the American context) has been that the nation's urban problems are very closely inter-related: the growth of metropolises, even megalopolises, and the decline of small towns, the migration of blacks to inner cities and of whites to the suburbs, are all so inter-related that a national policy of building up "intermediate-sized" cities is required. A second argument is that regional and urban development can no longer be viewed as separate issues, because the success of the former depends to some considerable degree upon the agglomeration economies resulting from the latter. This argument, put most forcibly by Richardson (1973), has already been reviewed in Chap. 5. It is reiterated here because the idea of a national urban strategy, setting out broad long-term targets for the major towns in a country, is one which accords closely with the evidence on growth centres reviewed in the body of this book. Certain countries (e.g. France, as we have seen) are moving in this direction. Such a direction appears much more sensible than the designation of isolated "growth centres".

SOME POLICY GUIDELINES

Whatever particular strategy of spatial discrimination is eventually decided upon, it must be remembered that areas of growth and of decline are two sides of the same coin. A joint solution is needed to the single problem of rural decline and urban growth and a programme of different but complementary and integrated policies must be worked out. Below we examine the selection of growth centres, the implementation of policy and the nature of political opposition. In each section, it is important to retain a horizon extending far beyond the immediate locality which is afforded favoured status.

(i) *The Selection of Growth Centres*

We have argued strongly in this book that there is no unambiguous entity termed "growth centre", no universally acceptable procedure for identifying "growth centres" and, in most circumstances, no irrefutable case for singling out individual isolated towns for preferential treatment to the total neglect of other centres in the region. An overall urban strategy, taking account of the needs and potential of *all* centres, is what is required. In moving towards such a strategy, the spatial pattern of a large number of indices should be examined, in order to make a better judgement of the growth possibilities of each centre. The chief criterion should not simply be growth potential, but what Klaassen has called "development worthiness"—and whether a place is worthy of development must depend in part upon the degree to which such development is consistent with wider regional or even national goals.

Four criteria in particular emerge from previous attempts to identify growth centres for planning purposes. First, location: an important factor is a town's inter- and intra-regional accessibility. Inter-regional accessibility is important if the centre is to be attractive for firms and migrants from outside the region. Upon its intra-regional accessibility will depend its ability to improve the employment opportunities of the residents of the region, be they commuters or migrants, and its value as a service centre for a wide area. Second, human resources: certainly the size, occupational range and level of skill of a town's labour force is particularly important in the generation of new development. So, too, is the quality of leadership, entrepreneurial ability and attitude to change of the town's political and business fraternity. Third, service provision: we have discussed in Chapters 5 and 7 the importance of urban amenities, in the widest sense, in the attraction of both new firms and migrants. An analysis should be made of the availability and, if possible, the spare capacity (Chap. 4) of services. Fourth, growth performance in the recent past. Such an index is likely to give a crude measure of a town's ability to foster the creation of new employment opportunities, since it will serve to some extent as a surrogate for a wide range of relevant factors. But, of course, the index is only valid to the extent that the reasons for recent growth remain valid. Growth in the recent past should probably be a necessary but certainly not a sufficient criterion in the selection of growth centres.

No specific proposals are put forward for the techniques to be used for measuring these various indices, nor for weighting their relative contribution. A number of relevant studies were reviewed in Chapter 1 and reference might profitably be made to the original sources. The point is that this exercise must necessarily be wholly inductive in the absence of a clearly defined growth-centre entity and should reflect the particular circumstances and problems of the region at issue. In most exercises it will be useful to employ a range of different criteria and to experiment with a variety of weighting procedures. The object is to generate a number of alternative strategies which would appear, *prima facie*, to channel new growth to suitable locations, but which subsequently require rigorous testing against a list of objectives, using an objectives–achievement matrix or some other evaluation procedure (Chadwick, 1971). This two-stage procedure—the generation of alternative strategies using development indices and the evaluation of the strategies in the context of weighted objectives—ensures that the degree to which individual towns become foci for new development depends in part upon their inherent attractiveness and in part upon their ability to contribute to wider goals. Goals of, for example, maximum growth in employment and of improving the quality of life in an egalitarian fashion (however defined) will require different strategies. It is in this dual context of growth potential and goals achievement that the concept of "development worthiness" has its meaning.

(ii) *Implementation*

A basic issue in implementing a growth-centre policy concerns whether active intervention is needed at all. Allen and Hermansen (1968) drew a distinction between "active" and "reinforcing" policies. The latter suffices if the present pattern of change is considered to be in the desired direction and if all that is needed is a modest acceleration of that pattern and a complementary programme of ensuring that the necessary public investment is undertaken at the appropriate time. More likely to be required, however, is an active policy of arresting present trends and of creating growth centres by actively seeking to influence the patterns of industrial and personal mobility. We will assume that an active policy is required and consider some policy issues relating to public investment, to the attraction of industry and of migrants, and to the people left behind.

First, there is a clear need to ensure that the pattern of *public investment* accords with the selected strategy. Expenditure on transport, housing, education facilities, etc., should reflect the new status accorded to the various settlements in the region. This is so obvious that it may seem a truism. But if the attitude and power of individual localities is such that wasteful expenditure is likely in areas scheduled for decline, then intervention from a higher level will be necessary. There may be a need for a regional budget—for some degree of financial autonomy at a level between local and national governments, so that the overall regional strategy can be fostered by a "pump-priming" programme of key investments—for example in technical training establishments or in housing for migrants. In any event, there is a need at the plan-making stage to identify the crucial "policy levers" upon which the successful implementation of the strategy depends.

Second is the necessity of attracting sufficient and suitable *employment opportunities* to the appropriate locations. In all probability there will be little latitude in the selection of suitable industry: few development agencies will feel free to turn away any potential industrialist. And to a considerable extent the perceived comparative advantages of the region and of the towns that it contains will decide its industrial future. But in seeking out new industry, there is scope for a selective deployment of resources and it is at this stage that consideration of the relative merits of different industries should be made. This involves an appraisal of the suitability of the growth centres for different sources of employment and an appreciation of the varying impact that different industries would make. We have seen (Chap. 6) that often the most substantial regional impact of new firms is via the labour market and, other things being equal, there is a strong case for seeking out labour-intensive firms. The establishment of a capital-intensive industrial complex is not only difficult to synchronise, but it may bring relatively little benefit to the region in terms of labour recruitment. And we have seen that apart from firms broadly in the engineering and metalworking sectors, spin-off to local suppliers is likely to be slight.

Regardless of the type of industry sought, it will be necessary to decide whether the chosen growth centres should be accorded preferential status in terms of the financial inducements offered to incoming industrialists. The alternative is for such inducements to be of constant magnitude throughout the region, with administrative action and the external economies of the growth centres being relied upon to steer growth to them. The Eire Industrial Development Authority (1972) has declared its intention of making extensive use between 1973 and 1977 of its powers to vary the level of grants available to industry, in order to induce industrialists to choose locations specified in the regional plans. British practice has tended to favour the second alternative, although the degree of discretion in the distribution of inducements to industry given by the 1972 Industry Act to the new Industrial Development Executives means that increasingly discriminatory policies can be pursued with varying degrees of openness. In most circumstances, however, the balance of advantages may lie with *not* having an explicit policy of this kind. If an industrialist is prepared to ignore the serviced industrial estates, labour-training facilities, housing availability, etc., of the growth centres, and opts for another location in the region, then there are likely to be good economic grounds (e.g. the availability of unskilled labour) for his so doing. And if it is clear that such industrialists will not be impeded in this decision or discriminated against in terms of financial inducements, then it will be a lot easier to "sell" the policy package to politicians from peripheral areas.

Third is a need for an explicit policy with regard to the *migration* that the identification of areas for growth and for decline inevitably implies. Two groups of people are particularly important—"spiralists" from other regions who can provide the skills and drive often lacking in a region which has suffered prolonged and selective outmigration, and "locals" living within the problem region but beyond effective commuting range of the growth centres. The possibility of attracting the former was discussed in Chapter 7. Here we examine those policies needed to attract the latter group of people to the growth centres, over and above the provision of sufficient employment there.

One key factor is housing. The "Hunt Report" on the problems of "intermediate areas" in Britain (Hunt, 1969) reviewed the schemes run by the British Government to facilitate migration from areas with high unemployment and found that the numbers taking advantage of such schemes were small and that the main impediment was housing availability. There was a need for much more flexibility by local authorities in making housing available to newcomers. This is a clear area for close co-operation between "exporting" and "reception" areas, in which the construction and letting of houses is a responsibility of both authorities and in which the needs of low-income potential migrants are borne in mind. And, coupled with the availability of reasonably priced housing, there should be an adequate reception mechanism designed to alleviate the problems inevitably felt by newcomers who may never have moved house before. It is clear that the private housing market alone is rarely adequate to sustain the scale of migration necessary for the social objectives of a growth-centre policy to be achieved.

Concerning the employment opportunities for migrants, it is rare that industrial expansion alone ensures that the unemployed and under-employed beyond the commuting hinterland benefit. There is a need to ensure that sufficient information about the jobs available flows to the problem areas and to the appropriate people in those areas, and that an efficient migrant placement service is in operation whereby potential migrants are assured employment before leaving home. Parallel to this is a requirement for a programme of vocational training and retraining, possibly carried out before departure in the area of origin, but financed from regional, not local, sources. The general point is that, as with housing, the growth-centre and depressed-area authorities must act as a single system, phasing a unified programme of expansion and decline, with careful reference to the employment and manpower available and to the skills that need to be imparted. The integration of housing and of employ-ment and manpower policies, and of policies pursued in growth centres and in declining areas, suggests that useful lessons might be learnt from the experience of the British new town and town expansion programmes, in which "exporting" and "reception" authorities have worked together in the construction and letting of houses and in the placement of migrants in new employment (Seeley, 1968).

Further to the requirement for integrated housing and manpower policies is a need for adequate financial assistance to make the move possible. This means redundancy payments, adequate grants for retrain-ing, travel allowances for trips to inspect houses and to attend interviews with employers, and resettlement allowances to defray the costs of moving and setting up home. In addition, Hansen (1970) has indicated in the American context a need for financial assistance to help pay off debts in the old location, indebtedness frequently being a powerful constraint on mobility. The cost of a programme of mobility assistance along these lines should be considered at the stage of evaluating alternative spatial strategies: in many cases it will be money well spent.

In addition to policies designed to ensure that the appropriate public investments, employment opportunities and personnel are attracted to the growth centres, there is a need for a package of *complementary policies* designed essentially for the benefit of those remaining in peripheral areas. One element of this package relates to the energetic promotion of those economic activities for which such areas enjoy comparative advantages. Tourism, recreation and retirement, agriculture and other primary activities, certain manufacturing activities not requiring an urban location: all can bring a significant injection of new employment in peripheral areas. But inevitably a major part of our policy package will stem from a frank acceptance of a reduced level of employment and of population. There will be a clear need to help those for whom retraining and migration does not provide the best solution, and to respond to the peculiar social problems arising from a declining and ageing population. This means subsidised service provision—expenditure designed to increase the mobility of people and of the services they require and to lower the effective thresholds at which service provision becomes possible. Such policies were outlined at the end of Chapter 4.

The general objective, then, is to help declining areas reach a new level of equilibrium with a minimum of friction. The focus in all this must be an emphasis on "human development", whether in the training and resettlement of migrants or the improvement of the health, welfare and educational facilities of those who stay behind. Planning for decline is not a subject that has received adequate attention or acceptance, in Britain at least, but if "people prosperity" remains the goal, then such planning is as challenging and as necessary as planning for growth.

(iii) *Political Pressures*

Of course, it would be wrong to imagine that the explicit acceptance of decline can be achieved without a good degree of political opposition. As Kuklinski (1970, p. 276) has stated: "Very few . . . growth centre policies have been implemented. The idea to channel growth opportunities to a selected number of places must generate resistance, especially at the local level. This is perhaps one of the problems of the sociology of regional development, how to extend the geographical horizon of local and regional authorities: how to induce the acceptance of national criteria on the regional level and regional criteria on the local level." Probably it is unrealistic, even undemocratic, to expect local politicians to accept "regional" goals at face-value. If the pursuit of such policies runs counter to the interests of their constituents, then it seems right that they should oppose them. The crucial issue is whether such policies do in fact run counter to the probable long-term interests of their constituents. It may be that the prestige and well-being of local politicians, administrators and businessmen depends to a greater degree upon growth *in situ* than does the well-being of many of their neighbours. In such circumstances, a policy of "people prosperity" will be hard to pursue.

The only solution to this, in a democratic society, seems to lie in a concerted programme of education designed to make clearer to all concerned the true nature of the costs and benefits that alternative plans for the future hold. This means much greater involvement of peripheral communities in the plan-making stage, so that a common set of goals might be arrived at, and the various practical possibilities for action fully explored and seen to be explored. The alternative, handing down a pre-packaged growth-centre strategy, is bound to lead to resentment in those areas not selected for growth. And if the representatives of aggrieved localities have any executive power, or some influence at a higher level, they will do their utmost to sabotage the plan. The prime need is to evolve a strategy which will bring net benefits to people throughout the region, even if this involves migration, and to publicise fully the real nature of the various alternatives. But there remains a need to know much more about the nature of the political processes involved in spatial planning and about the typical incidence of benefits of policies of spatial discrimination. Who decides? Who pays? Who benefits? All are important questions not fully resolved.

SOME SUGGESTIONS FOR RESEARCH

Finally, it may be useful to set out a number of topics upon which useful research might be undertaken. Most have been mentioned earlier in the text and are pulled together here, for convenience. Page numbers indicate an earlier reference, above. All topics relate to the effectiveness of growth-centre policies as tools of regional development. (For an alternative listing of research priorities in this field, see Kuklinski and Petrella, 1972, pp. 170–4.)

(i) *Innovation Diffusion* (Chap. 3)

1. To what extent are urban size and urban location relevant parameters in the diffusion of entrepreneurial innovations in modern manufacturing industry? Research might focus on the spread of new production techniques and processes and of managerial innovations (p. 66).
2. Is it possible to define a level in the urban hierarchy at which urban size ceases to be a prime determinator of the timing of the adoption of most entrepreneurial innovations, and at which urban location or other factors take over? (p. 63).
3. There is a need for more behavioural studies of the major actors involved in the diffusion of such innovations. How do they perceive the suitability of different locations? Upon what information do they reach decisions? (p. 68).

(ii) *Service Provision* (Chap. 4)

1. To what extent is the greater *per capita* cost of constructing and managing larger towns offset by the increased utility that urban size affords? (pp. 70–74).
2. What is the nature, magnitude and incidence of the costs and benefits involved in different policy packages designed to improve the quality of personal service provision in rural areas with static or declining populations? (pp. 85–86).

(iii) *Agglomeration Economies* (Chap. 5)

1. How far, and at what rate of decay, do the external economies arising from agglomeration extend away from an urban centre? (p. 112 and Fig. 5.6).
2. What kind of agglomeration economies are of most value to individual, specified industries? (p. 113).

3. How important is large urban size as a factor affecting the location and viability of the various activities which comprise the tertiary sector, and of the non-manufacturing activities of manufacturing firms (research and development, accountancy, etc.)? (pp. 106–9).

(iv) *Spread Effects* (Chap. 6)

1. In the diffusion of household innovations away from urban centres, what is the relative merit of proximity to a number of small centres compared with greater remoteness from a single much larger centre? (pp. 143–4).
2. Do Morrill's "waves of diffusion" have any empirical validity? Or is location in relation to neighbouring urban centres increasingly irrelevant in this context? (p. 142).
3. How is the decision reached by peripheral residents to take up employment with a growth-centre firm? How do they decide whether to commute or to migrate? (pp. 117, 143).
4. What is the spatial pattern of the multiplier effects arising from personal expenditure, by growth-centre workers, on services and goods *other* than typical retail commodities? (p. 141).
5. What is the spatial pattern of benefits arising from the public expenditure of income diverted into local taxes?
6. What affects the propensity of growth-centre firms to establish branch plants in neighbouring areas? (p. 136).
7. How permanent is the reluctance of most growth-centre firms to switch to local suppliers of materials and services? (pp. 134, 145).

(v) *Migration* (Chap. 7)

1. Who takes up employment opportunities created in growth centres? What proportion and what kind of jobs go to previously unemployed or underemployed residents of distressed areas? (p. 157).
2. To what extent is migration, say, 50 miles to a growth centre, less objectionable from a personal and social viewpoint, compared with a move of 500 miles to a capital city? (pp. 152–5).
3. Is it possible to establish "trade-off" preferences involving varying assumptions about the distance to migrate, the quality of the likely

employment opportunities, the nature of the urban destination, etc.? Can such preferences, if established, be built into a theoretical consideration of optimal patterns of spatial concentration? (pp. 152–5).

4. What is the relative role of urban size in the locational preferences of "spiralists"? (pp. 156–7).

(vi) *Implementation* (Chap. 8)

1. Why is the pursuit of growth afforded such significance by political and business élites in peripheral areas? (p. 170).
2. How far do the political leaders of peripheral communities effectively articulate the goals of their constituents? Do they perceive a conflict between "people" and "place" prosperity? (p. 170).
3. How best can we arrive at a true understanding and weighting of the goals of people in problem areas? (pp. 164–5).
4. In specific instances of the planned run-down of communities, what were the subsequent fortunes of the various people involved? Was "people prosperity" effectively achieved? (pp. 167–9).
5. What is the most appropriate administrative machinery for handling the employment, migration and investment issues which link areas of growth and decline? (pp. 168, 170).

Bibliography

This is not a comprehensive bibliography of growth-centre literature—indeed, given the ambiguities surrounding the concept, it cannot be. See Storey (1972) and Davy (1973) for more extensive listings. For the considerable French and Belgian literature on growth *poles*, see the bibliography by Darwent (1969). Good collections of papers on the subject appear in Hansen (1972a), Kuklinski (1972) and Kuklinski and Petrella (1972). Collections of relevant unpublished research papers have been produced by the United Nations Research Institute for Social Development (in Geneva), by the Center for Economic Development in the University of Texas at Austin and by the University of Kentucky, Lexington, Kentucky. Of these papers, only those cited in the text are listed below. Finally, two of those cited below, though clearly of great relevance, came too late to influence the text. They are Richardson (1973b) and EFTA (1974).

ABLER, R., ADAMS, J. S. and GOULD, P. (1972) *Spatial Organisation*, Prentice-Hall, London.
ALLEN, K. and HERMANSEN, T. (1968) Economic growth—regional problems and growth centres. In EFTA (1968).
ALLEN, K. and MACLENNAN, M. C. (1970) *Regional Problems and Policies in Italy and France*, Allen & Unwin, London.
ALONSO, W. (1970) What are new towns for? *Urban Studies*, **7**, 37–55.
ALONSO, W. (1971) The question of urban size. In *Urban and Regional Planning*, ed. A. G. WILSON, Pion, London.
ALONSO, W. and MEDRICH, E. (1972) Spontaneous growth centres in twentieth-century American urbanization. In Hansen (1972a).
AMBASSADE DE FRANCE (1968) *Regional Planning in France*, French Embassy, London.
ANTOINE, S. and WEILL, G. (1965) Les métropoles et leur région. *Urbanisme*, **89**, 11–19.
BATTY, M. (1969) The impact of a New Town: an application of the Garin–Lowry model. *Journal of the Town Planning Institute*, **55**, 428–35.
BAUCHET, P. (1961) La comptabilité économique régionale et son usage. *Economie appliquée*, **14**, January.

BEG, M. A. A. (1965) *Regional Growth Points in Economic Development (with Special Reference to West Virginia)*, Economic Development Series No. 8, West Virginia University.

BERGSMAN, J., GREENSTON, P. and HEALY, R. (1972) The agglomeration process in urban growth. *Urban Studies*, **9**, 263–88.

BERNARD, P. (1970) *Growth Poles and Growth Centres in Regional Development: Vol. III. Growth Poles and Growth Centres as Instruments of Regional Development and Modernization with Special Reference to Bulgaria and France*, Report No. 70.14, UNRISD, Geneva.

BERRY, B. J. L. (1965) Identification of declining regions: an empirical study of the dimensions of rural poverty. In *Areas of Economic Stress in Canada*, pp. 22–26, eds. W. D. WOOD and R. S. THOMAN, Industrial Relations Centre, Queen's University, Kingston, Ontario.

BERRY, B. J. L. (1968) *Metropolitan Area Definition: a Re-evaluation of Concept and Statistical Practice*, US Dept. of Commerce; Bureau of the Census. Working Paper No. 28, Washington, DC.

BERRY, B. J. L. (1969) Relationships between regional economic development and the urban system: the case of Chile. *Tijdschrift voor Economische en Sociale Geografie*, **60**, 283–307.

BERRY, B. J. L. (1970a) The geography of the United States in the year 2000. *Transactions, Institute of British Geographers*, **51**, 21–54.

BERRY, B. J. L. (1970b) Labour market participation and regional potential. *Growth and Change*, **1**, 3–10.

BERRY, B. J. L. (1972) Hierarchical diffusion: the basis of developmental filtering and spread in a system of cities. In Hansen (1972a).

BERRY, B. J. L. (1973) In *Geographic Perspectives and Urban Problems*, ed. F. HORTON, National Academy of Sciences, Washington, D.C.

BERRY, B. J. L. and NEILS, E. (1969) Location, size and shape of cities as influenced by environmental factors: the urban environment writ large. In *The Quality of the Urban Environment*, pp. 257–302, ed. H. S. PERLOFF, Johns Hopkins Press, Baltimore.

BERTRAND, Y. (1970) Aspects de la diffusion du développement dans un cadre régional à partir d'implantations industrielles récentes. *Bulletin de Conjoncture Régionale* (University of Rennes), **15**, 4.

BERTRAND, Y. and DUBOIS, M.-A. (1970) Effets d'implantations industrielles récentes (résultats d'enquêtes effectuées dans la région de Lannion). *Bulletin de Conjoncture Régionale* (University of Rennes), **15**, 1–2.

BEYERS, W. B. (1973) Growth centres and inter-industry linkage. *Proceedings Association of American Geographers*, **5**, 18–21.

BLACK, W. and SIMPSON, J. V. (1968) Growth centres in Ireland. *The Irish Banking Review*, Sept., 19–29.

BOAL, F. W. (1973) UK new towns: Northern Ireland. *Town and Country Planning*, **41**, 59–67.

BOUDEVILLE, J. R. (1966) *Problems of Regional Economic Planning*, Edinburgh University Press, Edinburgh.

BOUDEVILLE, J. R. (1968) *L'Espace et les Poles de Croissance*, Presse Universitaire de France, Paris.

BOUDEVILLE, J. R. (1972) *Aménagement du Territoire et Polarisation*, Genin, Paris.

VON BOVENTER, E. (1969) Determinants of migration into West German cities 1956–61, 1961–66. *Papers of Regional Science Association*, **23**, 53–62.

VON BOVENTER, E. (1970) Optimal spatial structure and regional development. *Kyklos*, **23**, 903–26.

VON BOVENTER, E. (1973) City size systems: theoretical issues, empirical regularities and planning guides. *Urban Studies*, **10**, 2, 145–62.

BROSSE, U. (1971) Regionalpolitische Konsequenzen aus einer Standortuntersuchung uber die Zulieferindustrie. *Informationen*, **21** (7), 177–83.

BROWN, A. J. (1972) *The Framework of Regional Economics in the United Kingdom*, University Press, Cambridge.

BROWN, L. A. (1968) *Diffusion Dynamics: A Review and Revision of the Quantitative Theory of a Spatial Diffusion of Innovations*, Lund Studies in Geography, Series B, No. 29, Gleerup, Lund.

BROWN, L. A. (1969) Diffusion of innovation: a macro view. *Economic Development and Cultural Change*, **17**, 189–211.

BROWN, L. A. (1972a) Diffusion process at the macro and meso scales: an update on a framework for future analysis. Unpublished paper, Department of Geography, Ohio State University.

BROWN, L. A. (1972b) Diffusion processes: recent developments and their relevance to growth pole effects. Unpublished paper, presented at the International Geographical Union Congress, Montreal.

BROWN, L. A. and COX, K. R. (1971) Empirical regularities in the diffusion of innovation. *Annals of Association of American Geographers*,**61**, 551–9.

BROWN, L. A. and LENTNEK, B. (1973) Innovation diffusion in a developing economy: a mesoscale view. *Economic Development and Cultural Change*, **21**, 274–92.

BUCHANAN, C. and PARTNERS (1968) *Regional Studies in Ireland*, An Foras Forbartha, Dublin.

BYLUND, E. (1972) Growth centre and administrative area problems within the framework of Swedish location policy. In Kuklinski (1972).

CAMERON, G. C. (1970) Growth areas, growth centres and regional conversion. *Scottish Journal of Political Economy*, **17**, 19–38.

CAMERON, G. C. and REID, G. L. (1966) *Scottish Economic Planning and the Attraction of Industry*, University of Glasgow Social and Economic Studies, Occasional Paper No. 6; Oliver & Boyd, Edinburgh.

CAROL, H. (1966) *Geographic Identification of Regional Growth Centres and Development Regions in Southern Ontario*, A Report to the Regional Development Branch, Department of Economics and Development, Province of Ontario, Toronto.

CARTER, H. (1971) The identification of growth points. In *The Application of Geographical Techniques to Physical Planning*, Proceedings of a Seminar and Lecture organised by An Foras Forbartha in association with the Geographical Society of Ireland. An Foras Forbartha, Dublin.

CASETTI, E., KING, L. J. and ODLAND, J. (1970) On the formal identification of growth poles in a spatial temporal context. Unpublished conference paper, Canadian Association of Geographers.

CASETTI, E., KING, L. J. and ODLAND, J. (1971) The formalization and testing of concepts of growth poles in a spatial context, *Environment and Planning*, **3**, 377–82.

CHADWICK, G. (1971) *A Systems View of Planning*, Pergamon, Oxford.

CLARK, C. (1945) The economic functions of a city in relation to its size. *Econometrica*, **13**, 97–113.

CLOUT, H. D. (1972) *Rural Geography: An Introductory Survey*, Pergamon, Oxford.

COHEN, Y. S. (1972) Diffusion of an innovation in an urban system: the spread of planned regional shopping centers in the United States 1949–1968. University of Chicago, Dept. of Geography Research Paper No. 140, Chicago.

COMMISSARIAT GÉNÉRAL DU PLAN (1966) *Fifth Plan: Economic and Social Development Plan (1966–1970)*, La Documentation Française, Paris.

CORDEY-HAYES, M. and MASSEY, D. B. (eds.) (1970) *An Operational Urban Development Model of Cheshire*, C.E.S., W.P. 64, Centre for Environmental Studies, London.

COURTNEY, D. S. (1972) *The Newfoundland Resettlement Program: a Case Study in Spatial Reorganisation and Growth Centre Strategy*, Dept. of Geography, Memorial University of Newfoundland.

CRAIN, R. L. (1966) Fluoridation: the diffusion of an innovation among cities. *Social Forces*, **44**, 467–76.

CRESSWELL, P. and THOMAS, R. (1972) Employment and population balance. In H. Evans (1972).

CZAMANSKI, S. (1964) A model of urban growth. *Papers, Regional Science Association*, **13**, 177–200.

DANIELS, P. W. (1969) Office decentralization from London—policy and practice. *Regional Studies*, **3**, 171–8.

DARWENT, D. F. (1969) Growth poles and growth centres in regional planning—a review. *Environment and Planning*, **1**, 5–32.

DATAR (1971) *Investment Incentives in France*, Délégation à l'Aménagement du Territoire et à l'Action Régionale, Paris.

DATAR (1973) *Aménagement du Territoire*, Délégation à l'Aménagement du Territoire et à l'Action Régionale, Paris.

DAVY, B. W. (1973) *Annotated Bibliography on Growth Centres*, Council of Planning Librarians, Exchange Bibliography No. 374–75, Monticello, Illinois.

DEPARTMENT OF ECONOMICS, IOWA STATE UNIVERSITY OF SCIENCE AND TECHNOLOGY (1966) *The Role of Growth Centers in Regional Economic Development* (4 vols.), Ames, Iowa. (For Vol. 1, see Fox (1966).)

DEPARTMENT OF THE ENVIRONMENT (1971) *Study of Rural Transport in West Suffolk*. Report by the Steering Group. Department of the Environment, London.

DIAMOND, D. (1972) New towns in their regional context. In H. Evans (1972).

DOCUMENTATION FRANÇAISE (1969) *Notes et Etudes Documentaires: Métropoles d'Equilibre et Aires Metropolitaines*, Documentation Française No. 3633, Paris.

DUNCAN, O. D. (1956) The optimum size of cities. In *Demographic Analysis*, eds. J. J. SPENGLER and O. D. DUNCAN, Free Press, Glencoe, Illinois.

EAST ANGLIA CONSULTATIVE COMMITTEE (1972) *Small Towns Study*, East Anglia Consultative Committee and the East Anglia Planning Council, Cambridge.

ECONOMIC CONSULTANTS (1971) *Strategic Plan for the South East: Studies Volume V*, HMSO, London.

EIRE (1964) *Ireland: Second Programme for Economic Expansion*, Stationery Office, Dublin.

EIRE (1969) *Ireland: Third Programme for Economic and Social Development 1969–72*, Stationery Office, Dublin.

EIRE: INDUSTRIAL DEVELOPMENT AUTHORITY (1972) *Regional Industrial Plans 1973–77*, Industrial Development Authority, Dublin.

EFTA (1968) *Regional Policy in EFTA: An Examination of the Growth Centre Idea*, Oliver & Boyd, Edinburgh.

EFTA (1974) *National Settlement Strategies: a framework for regional development*, Secretariat of the European Free Trade Association, Geneva.

EVANS, A. W. (1972) The pure theory of city size in an industrial economy. *Urban Studies*, **9**, 49–77.

EVANS, H. (ed.) (1972) *New Towns: the British Experience*, Charles Knight, London.

FOX, C. (1966) *The Role of Growth Centers in Regional Economic Development*, Dept. of Economics, State University of Science and Technology, Ames, Iowa.

FRIEDMANN, J. R. (1966) *Regional Development Policy: A Case Study of Venezuela*, MIT Press, Cambridge, Mass.

FRIEDMANN, J. R. (1969) *A General Theory of Polarized Development*, School of Architecture and Urban Planning, UCLA, Los Angeles (published also in Hansen (1972a)).

GAILE, G. L. (1973) Growth Center Theory: an analysis of its formal spatial-temporal aspects. Paper presented to Annual Meeting of the Southern California Academy of Sciences, California State University, Long Beach.

GASKIN, M. *et al.* (1969) *North East Scotland: A Survey of its Development Potential*, HMSO, Edinburgh.

GOLDSMITH, H. F. and COPP, J. H. (1964) Metropolitan dominance and agriculture, *Rural Sociology*, **29**, 385–95.

GOODALL, B. (1972) *The Economics of Urban Areas*, Pergamon, Oxford.

GOULD, P. and TORNQVIST, G. (1971) Information, innovation and acceptance. In *Information Systems for Regional Development—A Seminar*, eds. T. HAGERSTRAND and A. R. KUKLINSKI, Lund Studies in Geography, Ser. B, No. 37, Gleerup, Lund.

GREEN, R. J. (1971) *Country Planning*, University of Manchester Press, Manchester.

GREENWOOD, M. J. (1969) An analysis of determinants of geographic labour mobility in the US. *Review of Economics and Statistics*, **51**, 189–94.

GREENWOOD, M. J. (1970) Lagged response in the decision to migrate. *Journal of Regional Science*, **10**, 375–84.

GRIEVE, R. (1972) Problems and objectives in the Highlands and Islands. In *The Remoter Rural Areas of Britain*, eds. J. ASHTON and W. H. LONG, Oliver & Boyd, Edinburgh.

GUPTA, S. P. and HUTTON, J. P. (1968) *Economies of Scale in Local Government Services*, Royal Commission on Local Government in England, Research Studies, No. 3, HMSO, London.

HAGERSTRAND, T. (1952) *The Propagation of Innovation Waves*, Lund Studies in Geography, Ser. B, Human Geography, No. 4, Gleerup, Lund.

HAGERSTRAND, T. (1965) On the Monte Carlo simulation of diffusion. *European Journal of Sociology*, **6**, 43–67.

HAGERSTRAND, T. (1967) *Innovation Diffusion as a Spatial Process* (translated and postscript by A. R. Pred), University of Chicago Press, Chicago.

HALE, C. W. (1967) The mechanism of the spread effect in regional development. *Land Economics*, **43**, 434–44.

HALL, R. K. (1972) The movement of offices from Central London. *Regional Studies*, **6**, 385–92.

HANNAN, D. F. (1969) Migration motives and migration differentials among Irish rural youth. *Sociologia Ruralis*, **9**, 195–220.

HANSEN, N. M. (1967) Development pole theory in a regional context. *Kyklos*, **20**, 709–27.

HANSEN, N. M. (1968) *French Regional Planning*, University Press, Edinburgh.

HANSEN, N. M. (1970) *Rural Poverty and the Urban Crisis: A Strategy for Regional Development*, Indiana University Press, Bloomington.

HANSEN, N. M. (1971) *Intermediate-size Cities as Growth Centers*, Praeger, New York.

HANSEN, M. M. (ed.) (1972a) *Growth Centers in Regional Economic Development*, The Free Press (Macmillan), New York.

HANSEN, N. M. (1972b) Criteria for a growth centre policy. In Kuklinski (1972).

HANSEN, N. M. (1972c) Growth center policy in the United States. In Hansen (1972a).

HANSEN, W. L. and TIEBOUT, C. M. (1963) An inter-sectoral flows analysis of the Californian economy. *Review of Economics and Statistics*, **45**, 409–18.

HARDMAN, SIR H. (1973) *The Dispersal of Government Work from London*, Cmnd 5322, HMSO, London.

HARRIS, AMELIA I. and CLAUSEN, R. (1966) *Labour Mobility in Great Britain, 1953–63*, Government Social Survey, HMSO, London.

HAUTREUX, J. (1966) Le rôle des métropoles d'équilibre dans l'armature urbaine. *Revue Juridique et Economique du Sud-Ouest*, **4**, 791–809.

HAUTREUX, J., LECOURT, and ROCHEFORT (1963) *Le Niveau Supérieur* (see HANSEN (1968)).

HERMANSEN, T. (1972a) Development poles and related theories: a synoptic review. In Hansen (1972a).

HERMANSEN, T. (1972b) Development poles and development centres in national and regional development, elements of a theoretical framework. In Kuklinski (1972).

HIGGINS, B. (1972) Regional interaction, the frontier and economic growth. In Kuklinski (1972).

HIGHLANDS AND ISLANDS DEVELOPMENT BOARD (1967– …) *First Report (1966)* (and annually thereafter), HIDB, Inverness.

HIRSCH, W. Z. (1959) Expenditure implications of metropolitan growth and consolidation. *Review of Economics and Statistics*, **41**, 232–41.

HIRSCH, W. Z. (1968) The supply of urban public services. In *Issues in Urban Economics*, eds. H. S. PERLOFF and L. WINGO, Baltimore.

HIRSCHMAN, A. O. (1958) *The Strategy of Economic Development*, Yale University Press, New Haven and London.

HOCH, I. (1972) Income and city size. *Urban Studies*, **9**, 299–328.

HODGE, G. (1965) The prediction of trade center viability in the Great Plains. *Papers of Regional Science Association*, **15**, 87–115.

HODGE, G. (1966) *The Identification of "Growth Poles" in Eastern Ontario*, a Report to the Ontario Department of Economics and Development, Ontario.

HODGE, G. (1968) Urban structure and regional development. *Proceedings of Regional Science Association*, **21**, 101–24.

HOLLINGSWORTH, T. H. (1970) *Migration: a Study based on Scottish Experience between 1939 and 1964*, University of Glasgow, Social and Economic Studies, Occasional Paper No. 12, Oliver & Boyd, Edinburgh.

HOLMES, J. (1968) *The Moray Firth: A Plan for Growth in a Sub-region of the Scottish Highlands* (Holmes Report), Highlands and Islands Development Board, Inverness.

HOOVER, E. M. (1969) Some old and new issues in regional development. In *Backward Areas in Advanced Countries*, ed. E. A. G. ROBINSON, Macmillan, London.

HOOVER, E. M. (1971) *An Introduction to Regional Economics*, A. A. Knopf, New York.

HOUSE, J. W. *et al.* (1968) Mobility of the northern business manager. *Papers on Migration and Mobility in Northern England*, No. 8, Dept. of Geography, University of Newcastle-upon-Tyne.

HUDSON, J. C. (1969) Diffusion in a central place system. *Geographical Analysis*, **1**, 45–58.

HUGHES, J. T. (1967) Economic aspects of local government reform. *Scottish Journal of Political Economy*, **14**, 118–37.

HUGHES, J. T. and KOZLOWSKI, J. (1968) Threshold analysis—an economic tool for town and regional planning. *Urban Studies*, **5**, 132–43.

HUNT, SIR JOSEPH (1969) *Report of a Committee on the Intermediate Areas*, Cmnd 3998, HMSO, London.

IRISH BANKING REVIEW (1972) Regional industrial planning. *Irish Banking Review*, June, 11–17.

JACKSON, M. and NOLAN, M. (1971) Threshold analysis: concept, criticisms and current usage. *Chartered Surveyor*, **104**, 288–93.

JACKSON, M. and NOLAN, M. (1973) Threshold analysis: II. Urban growth and programming. *Chartered Surveyor*, **105**, 308–15.

JAMES, B. G. S. (1964) The incompatibility of industrial and trading cultures: a critical appraisal of the growth point concept. *Journal of Industrial Economics*, **13**, 90–94.

JANSEN, A. C. M. (1970) The value of growth pole theory for economic geography. *Tijdschrift voor Economische en Sociale Geografie*, **61**, 67–76.

JANSEN, C. J. (1968) *Social Aspects of Internal Migration: a Research Report*, University of Bath.

JANSEN, C. J. (1969) Some sociological aspects of migration. In *Migration*, ed. J. A. JACKSON, Sociological Studies 2, University Press, Cambridge.

JOHNSTON, T. L., BUXTON, N. K. and MAIR, D. (1971) *Structure and Growth of the Scottish Economy*, Collins, London and Glasgow.

KARASKA, G. J. (1969) Manufacturing linkages in the Philadelphia economy: some evidence of external agglomeration forces. *Geographical Analysis* **1**, 354–69.

KEEBLE, D. E. (1967) Models of economic development. In *Socio-Economic Models in Geography*, eds. R. J. CHORLEY and P. HAGGETT, Methuen, London.

KEEBLE, D. E. (1969) Local industrial linkage and manufacturing growth in Outer London. *Town Planning Review*, **40**, 163–88.

KEEBLE, D. E. (1971) Employment mobility in Britain. In *Spatial Policy Problems of the British Economy*, eds. M. CHISHOLM and G. MANNERS, University Press, Cambridge.

KEEBLE, D. E. (1972) Industrial movement and regional development in the United Kingdom. *Town Planning Review,* **43,** 3–25.

KEEBLE, D. E. and HAUSER, D. P. (1972) Spatial analysis of manufacturing growth in outer South-east England, 1960–1967. *Regional Studies,* **6,** 11–36.

KLAASSEN, L. H. (1970) Growth poles in economic theory and policy. In *A Review of the Concepts and Theories of Growth Poles and Growth Centres,* eds. T. HERMANSEN *et al.,* United Nations Research Institute for Social Development, Geneva.

KLAASSEN, L. H. (1972) *Growth Poles in Economic Theory and Policy.* In Kuklinski and Petrella (1972).

KOTTER, H. (1962) Economic and social implications of rural industrialisation. *International Labour Review,* **86,** 1–14.

KOZLOWSKI, J. (1968) Threshold theory and the sub-regional plan. *Town Planning Review,* **39,** 99–116.

KOZLOWSKI, J. and HUGHES, J. T. (1967) Urban threshold theory and analysis. *Journal of Town Planning Institute,* **53,** 55–60.

KOZLOWSKI, J., HUGHES, J. T. and BROWN, R. (1972) *Threshold Analysis—A Quantitative Planning Method,* Architectural Press, London.

KRIM, A. J. (1967) *The Innovation and Diffusion of the Street Railway in North America,* MA Thesis, University of Chicago (reported in Berry and Neils (1969)).

KUEHN, J. A. and BENDER, L. D. (1969) An empirical identification of growth centers. *Land Economics,* **45,** 435–43.

KUKLINSKI, A. R. (1970) Regional development, regional policies and regional planning: problems and issues. *Regional Studies,* **4,** 269–78.

KUKLINSKI, A. R. (ed.) (1972) *Growth Poles and Growth Centres in Regional Planning,* Mouton, Paris and The Hague.

KUKLINSKI, A. R. and PETRELLA, R. (eds.) (1972) *Growth Poles and Regional Policies,* UNRISD, Mouton, Paris and The Hague.

KUPPER, U. I. (1969) Socio geographic aspects of industrial growth at Shannon. *Irish Geography,* **6,** 14–29.

LABER, G. (1972) Employment growth and changes in unemployment at the county level. In Hansen (1972a).

LAMPARD, E. E. (1955) The history of cities in economically advanced areas. *Economic Development and Cultural Change,* **3,** 81–136.

LANSING, J. B. and MUELLER, E. (1967) *The Geographic Mobility of Labour,* Ann Arbor: Survey Research Center, University of Michigan.

LASUEN, J. R. (1969) On growth poles. *Urban Studies,* **6,** 137–61.

LASUEN, J. R. (1973) Urbanisation and development—the temporal interaction between geographical and sectoral clusters. *Urban Studies,* **10,** 163–88.

LEAN, W. (1969) An economist's note on the validity of urban threshold theory. *Journal of Town Planning Institute,* **55,** 311.

LEVER, W. F. (1972a) Industrial movement, spatial association and functional linkages. *Regional Studies,* **6,** 371–84.

LEVER, W. F. (1972b) Regional multipliers and demand leakages. Unpublished paper presented to the Urban Studies Conference on Regional Policy, Oxford.

LEWIN, A. (1965) Caractères originaux des métropoles d'équilibre. *Urbanisme,* **89,** 26–34.

LEWIS, J. C. and PRESCOTT, J. R. (1972) Urban regional development and growth centers: an econometric study. *Journal of Regional Science*, **12**, 57–70.

LICHFIELD, N. and ASSOCIATES (1967) *Report and Advisory Outline Plan for the Limerick Region. Vol. II: Advisory Outline Plan*, Stationery Office, Dublin.

LIVESEY, F. (1972) Industrial complexity and regional economic development. *Town Planning Review*, **43**, 225–42.

LLOYD, P. E. and DICKEN, P. (1972) *Location in Space: A Theoretical Approach to Economic Geography*, Harper & Row, New York.

LOCAL GOVERNMENT OPERATIONAL RESEARCH UNIT (1968) *Royal Commission on Local Government in England: Research Studies 4: Performance and Size of Local Education Authorities*, HMSO, London.

LOGAN, M. I. (1970) The spatial dimensions of economic development: the case of the Upper Midwest. *Regional Studies*, **4**, 117–25.

LOMAX, K. S. (1943) The relation between expenditure per head and size of population of county boroughs in England and Wales. *Journal of the Royal Statistical Society*, **106**, 51–59.

LOWRY, I. S. (1966) *Migration and Metropolitan Growth: Two Analytical Models*, Chandler Publishing Co., San Francisco.

LUCEY, D. I. F. and KALDOR, D. R. (1969) *Rural Industrialization: the Impact of Industrialization on Two Rural Communities in Western Ireland*, G. Chapman, London.

LUTTRELL, W. F. (1972) Industrial complexes and regional economic development in Canada. In Kuklinski (1972).

MCCRONE, G. (1969) *Regional Policy in Britain*, Allen & Unwin, London.

MCVOY, E. C. (1940) Patterns of diffusion in the United States. *American Sociological Review*, **5**, 219–27.

MALISZ, B. (1969) Implications of threshold theory for urban and regional planning. *Journal of Town Planning Institute*, **55**, 108–10.

MANN, M. (1973) *Workers on the Move*, University Press, Cambridge.

MATTHEW, R. H. (1964) *Belfast Regional Survey and Plan 1962*, HMSO, Belfast.

MATTHEW, R. H. and JOHNSON-MARSHALL, P. (1968) *Central Lancashire, Study for a City: Consultants' Proposals for Designation*, HMSO for Ministry of Housing & Local Government, London.

MATTHEW, R. H., WILSON, T. and PARKINSON, J. (1970) *The Northern Ireland Development Programme 1970–75*, HMSO, Belfast.

MEIER, R. L. (1962) *A Communications Theory of Urban Growth*, MIT Press, Cambridge, Mass.

MILLIGAN, J. (1973) The North Sea oil game. *Town and Country Planning*, **14**, 363–7.

MILLS, E. S. (1972) Welfare aspects of national policy toward city sizes. *Urban Studies*, **9**, 117–24.

MILNE, N. D. (1970) *Selecting Growth Centers*. Discussion Paper No. 6, Program on the role of growth centres in regional economic development. Center for Economic Development, University of Texas at Austin.

MINISTRY OF HOUSING AND LOCAL GOVERNMENT (1968) *Impact on North East Lancashire: Central Lancashire New Town Proposal*, HMSO, London.

MISRA, R. P. (1972) Growth poles and growth centres in the context of India's urban and regional development problems. In Kuklinski (1972).

MORRILL, R. (1968) Waves of spatial diffusion. *Journal of Regional Science*, **8**, 1–18.

MORRILL, R. L. (1973a) On the size and spacing of growth centers. *Growth and Change*, **4**, 21–24.

MORRILL, R. L. (1973b) Fundamental issues concerning future settlement in America. In *Geographic Perspectives and Urban Problems*, ed. F. HORTON, National Academy of Sciences, Washington, D.C.

MOSELEY, M. J. (1972) The spatial impact of growth centres: case studies in Brittany and East Anglia. Unpublished Ph.D. thesis, University of Reading.

MOSELEY, M. J. (1973a) The impact of growth centres in rural regions. I. An analysis of spatial "patterns" in Brittany. *Regional Studies*, **7**, 57–75.

MOSELEY, M. J. (1973b) The impact of growth centres in rural regions. II. An analysis of spatial "flows" in East Anglia. *Regional Studies*, **7**, 77–94.

MOSELEY, M. J. (1973c) Some problems of small expanding towns. *Town Planning Review*, **44**, 263–78.

MOSELEY, M. J. (1973d) Growth centres—a shibboleth? *Area*, **5**, 143–50.

MOSELEY, M. J. and TOWNROE, P. M. (1973) Linkage adjustment following industrial movement. *Tijdshrift voor Economische en Sociale Geographie*, **64**, 137–44.

MYRDAL, G. M. (1957) *Economic Theory and Underdeveloped Regions*, Gerald Duckworth, London.

NATIONAL ECONOMIC DEVELOPMENT OFFICE (1971) *The Future Pattern of Shopping*, Committee for the Distributive Trades, NEDO, HMSO, London.

NATIONAL INDUSTRIAL AND ECONOMIC COUNCIL (EIRE) (1965) *Comments on Report of Committee on Development Centres and Industrial Estates*, Stationery Office, Dublin.

NATIONAL INDUSTRIAL AND ECONOMIC COUNCIL (EIRE) (1968) *Report on Industrial Adaptation and Development*, Stationery Office, Dublin.

NATIONAL INDUSTRIAL AND ECONOMIC COUNCIL (EIRE) (1969) *Report on Physical Planning*, Stationery Office, Dublin.

NEUTZE, G. M. (1967) *Economic Policy and the Size of Cities*, Augustus M. Kelly, New York.

NEWCOMBE, V. Z. (1969) Creating an industrial development pole in southern Italy. *Journal of Town Planning Institute*, **55**, 157–61.

NEWMAN, J. (1967) *New Dimensions in Regional Planning: A Case Study of Ireland* An Foras Forbartha, Dublin.

NICHOLLS, W. H. (1961) Industrialization, factor markets and agricultural development. *Journal of Political Economy*, **69**, 319–40.

NICHOLS, V. (1969) Growth poles: an evaluation of their propulsive effect. *Environment and Planning*, **1**, 193–208.

NORFOLK COUNTY COUNCIL (1972) *Interim Settlement Policy*, Norfolk County Planning Dept., County Hall, Norwich.

NORTHAM, R. M. (1969) Population size, relative location and declining urban centres: conterminous United States, 1940–1960. *Land Economics*, **45**, 313–22.

OECD SOCIAL AFFAIRS DIVISION (1968) *Measures of Adjustment of Rural Manpower to Industrial Work and Urban Areas*, OECD, Paris.

O'FARRELL, P. N. (1970) Regional development in Ireland. Problem of goal formulation and objective specification. *Economic and Social Review*, **2**, 71–92.

O'FARRELL, P. N. (1971) The regional problem in Ireland: some reflections upon development strategy. *Economic and Social Review*, **2**, 453–80.

OHUIGINN, P. (1972) *Regional Development and Industrial Location in Ireland*, An Foras Forbartha, Dublin.

O'NEILL, H. B. (1971) *Spatial Planning in the Small Economy: A Case Study of Ireland*, Praeger, New York.
PARKER, A. J. (1972) Ireland: a consideration of the 1971 census of population. *Area*, **4**, 31–38.
PARKER, A. J. (1973) Work for Irishmen: regional planning and employment creation in the Irish Republic. *Geographical Magazine*, Feb. 338–40.
PARR, J. B. (1965) The nature and function of growth poles in economic development. Mimeographed paper, presented at a meeting of the Assoc. of American Geographers, Columbus, Ohio, April.
PARR, J. B. (1966) Outmigration and the depressed area problem. *Land Economics*, **42**, 149–59.
PARR, J. B. (1972a) Regional economic change and regional spatial structure. Paper to the Second Advanced Studies Institute in Regional Science, Karlsruhe, July.
PARR, J. B. (1972b) Growth poles, central place analysis and regional development. Paper to the Twelfth European Congress of the Regional Science Association, Rotterdam, September.
PEDERSEN, P. O. (1970) Innovation diffusion in a national urban system. The case of Chile. *Geographical Analysis*, **2**, 203–54.
PEDERSEN, P. O. (1971) Innovation diffusion in urban systems. In *Information Systems for Regional Development—A Seminar*, eds. T. HAGERSTRAND and A. R. KUKLINSKI, Lund Studies in Geography Ser. B, No. 37, Gleerup, Lund.
PENOUIL, M. (1969) An appraisal of regional development policy in the Aquitaine region. In E. A. G. ROBINSON (ed.), *Backward Areas in Advanced Countries*, Macmillan, London.
PERROUX, F. (1950) Economic space, theory and applications. *Quarterly Journal of Economics*, **64**, 90–97.
PERROUX, F. (1955) Note sur la notion des pôles de croissance. *Economie Appliquée,* **1** and **2**, 307–20.
PERROUX, F. (1964) *L'Economie de XX Siècle*, Press Universitaire de France, Paris.
PIATIER, A. (1965) Les fonctions de polarisation. *Urbanisme* **89**, 20–25.
PRED, A. R. (1965) Industrialisation, initial advantage and American metropolitan growth. *Geographical Review*, **55**, 158–85.
PRED, A. R. (1966) *The Spatial Dynamics of U.S. Urban-Industrial Growth 1800–1914: Interpretive and Theoretical Essays*, MIT Press, Cambridge, Mass.
PRED, A. R. (1967) see Hagerstrand (1967).
PYLE, G. F. (1969) The diffusion of cholera in the United States in the nineteenth century. *Geographical Analysis*, **1**, 59–75.
REGULSKI, J. (1972) Development poles theory and its application in Poland. In Kuklinski (1972).
RHODES, J. and KAN, A. (1971) *Office Dispersal and Regional Policy*, Dept. of Applied Economics Occasional Paper No. 30, University Press, Cambridge.
RIAGAIN, P. O. (1971) The selection of village growth points. In *The Application of Geographical Techniques to Physical Planning*, Proceedings of a Seminar and Lecture organised by An Foras Forbartha, Dublin.
RICHARDSON, H. W. (1969) *Regional Economics*, Weidenfeld & Nicolson, London.
RICHARDSON, H. W. (1971) Regional development policy in Spain. *Urban Studies,* **8**, 39–53.

RICHARDSON, H. W. (1972) Optimality in city size, systems of cities and urban policy: a sceptic's view. *Urban Studies*, **9**, 29–48.

RICHARDSON, H. W. (1973a) *Regional Growth Theory*, Macmillan, London.

RICHARDSON, H. W. (1973b) *The Economics of Urban Size*, Saxon House Studies, D. C. Heath & Co.

RICHTER, C. E. (1969) The impact of industrial linkages on geographic association. *Journal of Regional Sciences*, **9**, 19–28.

RICHTER, C. E. (1970) Systematic relationship between industrial linkages and the agglomeration of manufacturing industries. *Review of Regional Studies*, **1**, 37–48.

RIKKINEN, K. (1968) Change in village and rural population with distance from Duluth. *Economic Geography*, **44**, 312–25.

ROBINSON, G. and SALIH, K. B. (1971) The spread of development around Kuala Lumpur: a methodology for an exploratory test of some assumptions of the growth pole model. *Regional Studies*, **5**, 303–14.

RODWIN, L. (1970) *Nations and Cities*, Houghton Mifflin, New York.

ROYAL COMMISSION ON LOCAL GOVERNMENT IN ENGLAND (1969) *Volume III: Research Appendices*, Cmnd. 4040—II, HMSO, London.

RUTMAN, G. L. (1970) Migration and economic opportunities in west Virginia: a statistical analysis. *Rural Sociology*, **35**, 206–17.

RUTTAN, V. W. (1955) The impact of urban-industrial development on agriculture in the Tennessee Valley and the south-east. *Journal of Farm Economics*, **37**, 38–56.

RYAN, B. (1970) The criteria for selecting growth centers in Appalachia. *Proceedings Association of American Geographers*, **2**, 118–23.

SALT, J. (1967) The impact of the Ford and Vauxhall plants on the employment situation of Merseyside, 1962–1965. *Tijdschrift voor Economische en Sociale Geografie*, **58**, 255–64.

SANT, M. E. C. (1974) *Industrial Movement and Regional Development* (in preparation), Pergamon Press, Oxford.

SCHWIND, P. J. (1971) *Migration and Regional Development in the United States 1950–1960*, Dept. of Geography Research Paper No. 133, University of Chicago.

SCOTTISH COUNCIL (DEVELOPMENT AND INDUSTRY) (1952) *Report of the Committee on Local Development in Scotland* (*Cairncross Report*), HMSO, Edinburgh.

SCOTTISH COUNCIL (DEVELOPMENT AND INDUSTRY) (1961) *Report of the Committee of Inquiry into the Scottish Economy* (*Toothill Report*), HMSO, Edinburgh.

SCOTTISH DEVELOPMENT DEPT. (1963) *Central Scotland: a Programme for Development and Growth*, Cmnd 2188, HMSO, Edinburgh.

SCOTTISH DEVELOPMENT DEPT. (1966) *The Lothians Regional Survey and Plan* (2 vols.), HMSO, Edinburgh.

SCOTTISH DEVELOPMENT DEPT. (1968a) *The Grangemouth/Falkirk Regional Survey and Plan* (2 vols.), HMSO, Edinburgh.

SCOTTISH DEVELOPMENT DEPT. (1968b) *Central Borders: a Plan for Expansion* (2 vols.), HMSO, Edinburgh.

SCOTTISH DEVELOPMENT DEPT. (1970a) *A Strategy for South West Scotland*, HMSO, Edinburgh.

SCOTTISH DEVELOPMENT DEPT. (1970b) *Report for 1969*, Cmnd. 4313, HMSO, Edinburgh (Reports are annual, and are published the following year).

SCOTTISH OFFICE (1964) *Development & Growth in Scotland 1963–64*, Cmnd 2440, HMSO, Edinburgh.

SCOTTISH OFFICE (1966) *The Scottish Economy 1965–1970*, Cmnd 2864, HMSO, Edinburgh.

SEARS, D. W. and DYMSZA, R. B. (1969) Growth pole theory: a test. Unpublished paper. Agricultural Experiment Station, Cornell University, Ithaca, New York.

SEELEY, I. H. (1968) *Planned Expansion of Country Towns*, George Godwin, London.

SEMPLE, R. K., GAUTHIER, H. L. and YOUNGMAN, C. E. (1972) Growth poles in São Paulo, Brazil. *Annals of Association of American Geographers*, **62**, 591–9.

SHACKLEFORD, J. (1970) *On Thresholds, Take-offs and Spurts: a Place for SMSA's in Growth Center Strategy.* Discussion Paper No. 27, Program on the Role of Growth Centers in Regional Economic Development, University of Kentucky.

SMITH, B. M. D. (1970) Industrial overspill in theory and practice. The case of the West Midlands. *Urban Studies*, **7**, 189–204.

SMITH, D. M. (1971) *Industrial Location: an Economic Geographical Analysis*, John Wiley, New York and London.

SOMERMEIJER, W. H. (1961) Een analyse van de binnenlandse migratie in Nederland tot 1947 en van 1948–1957. *Statistiche en Econometrische Ondersoekingen*, pp. 115–74.

STANBACH, T. M. and KNIGHT, R. V. (1970) *The Metropolitan Economy: The Process of Employment Expansion*, Columbia Univ. Press, New York.

STONE, P. A. (1972) The economics of the form and organisation of cities. *Urban Studies*, **9**, 329–46.

STONE, P. A. (1973) *The Structure, Size and Costs of Urban Settlements*, University Press, Cambridge.

STOREY, K. J. (1972) Growth poles and growth centres: a selected bibliography, Unpublished. Dept. of Geography, Memorial University of Newfoundland.

STREIT, M. E. (1969) Spatial associations and economic linkages between industries. *Journal of Regional Science*, **9**, 177–88.

SVIMEZ, (1967) *Ricerca sui costi d'insediamento*, Rome.

TAYLOR, R. C. (1969) Migration and motivation: a study of determinants and types. In *Migration*, ed. J. A. JACKSON, Sociological Studies 2, Cambridge University Press.

TAYLOR, W. L. (1973) Scotland: New Town progress. *Town and Country Planning*, **41**, 177–80.

THOMAS, M. D. (1972) The regional problem, structural change and growth pole theory. In Kuklinski (1972).

THOMPSON, W. R. (1965) *A Preface to Urban Economics*, Johns Hopkins Press, Baltimore.

THOMPSON, W. R. (1968) Internal and external factors in the development of urban economics. In *Issues in Urban Economics*, eds. H. S. PERLOFF and L. WINGO JR., Johns Hopkins Press, Baltimore.

THOMPSON, W. R. (1972) The national system of cities as an object of public policy. *Urban Studies*, **9**, 99–116.

TOLOSA, H. and REINER, T. A. (1970) The economic programming of a system of planned poles. *Economic Geography*, **46**, 449–57.

TORNQUIST, G. (1967) *Growth of TV Ownership in Sweden 1956–1965: An Empirical-Theoretical Study*, Almquist & Wiksell, Stockholm.

TORNQUIST, G. (1968) Flows of information and the location of economic activities. *Lund Studies in Geography*, Ser. B, No. 30, Gleerup, Lund.

TOWNROE, P. M. (1970) Industrial linkage, agglomeration and external economies. *Journal of Town Planning Institute*, **56,** 18–20.

TURNER, D. M. (1966) The interrelationship of urban and rural communities. Unpublished Ph.D. thesis, Univ. of Cambridge.

TURNOCK, D. (1966) Lochaber: West Highland growth point. *Scottish Geographical Magazine*, **82,** 17–28.

TURNOCK, D. (1970) *Patterns of Highland Development*, Macmillan, London.

UNITED STATES DEPT. OF AGRICULTURE (1961) *Rural Industrialization: A Summary of Five Studies*, Agricultural Information Bulletin No. 252, Washington, D.C.

Urbanisme (1965) Special Issue, No. 89. Métropoles d'équilibre.

VANDERKAMP, J. (1971) Migration flows, their determinants and the effects of return migration. *Journal of Political Economy*, **79,** 1012–31.

VINEY, M. (ed.) (1969) *Seven Seminars: An Appraisal of Regional Planning in Ireland*, An Foras Forbartha, Dublin.

WARREN, K. (1972) Scotland. In *Regional Development in Britain*, ed. G. MANNERS *et al.*, John Wiley, London.

WEINAND, H. (1969) The spatial repercussions of economic growth and development: a case study of Nigeria. Unpublished M.Sc. (Geography) Thesis, Univ. of Wisconsin.

WEINAND, H. (1973) Some spatial aspects of economic development in Nigeria. *Journal of Developing Areas*, **7,** 247–64.

WILSON, T. (1965) *Economic Development in Northern Ireland*, Cmnd. 479, HMSO, Belfast.

WRIGHT, M. (1967) *Advisory Regional Plan & Final Report: the Dublin Region* (2 vols.), Stationery Office, Dublin.

YAPA, L., POLESE, M. and WOLPERT, J. (1969) Interdependence of commuting and migration. *Proceedings Association of American Geographers*, **1,** 163–8.

YEATES, M. H. and LLOYD, P. E. (1969) *Impact of Industrial Incentives: Southern Georgia Bay Region, Ontario*, Geographical Paper No. 44, Policy and Planning Branch, Dept. of Energy, Mines and Resources, Ottawa, Canada.

Index